Faith Out Loud

A Cumberland Presbyterian
YOUTH RESOURCE
Volume 4, Quarter 4

Discipleship Ministry Team
Ministry Council
Cumberland Presbyterian Church

April 2015

8207 Traditional Place
Cordova (Memphis), Tennessee 38016

©2015 Discipleship Ministry Team

All Rights Reserved. No part of this book may be reproduced or transmitted in any form or by any means, electronic or mechanical, including photocopying, recording, or by any information storage or retrieval system, without permission in writing from the publisher with the single exception that purchase of this curriculum grants the purchaser the right to copy and distribute student handouts within each lesson for use in their local church. For information address Discipleship Ministry Team, Cumberland Presbyterian Center, 8207 Traditional Place, Cordova (Memphis), Tennessee, 38016-7414.

The Discipleship Ministry Team of the Ministry Council of the Cumberland Presbyterian Church is the successor organization to the Board of Christian Education of the Cumberland Presbyterian Church.

Funded, in part, by your contributions to Our United Outreach.

First Edition (Revised) 2015

Published by The Discipleship Ministry Team, CPC
Memphis, Tennessee

ISBN-13: 978-0692414903
ISBN-10: 0692414908

We want to hear from you.
Please send your comments about this curriculum to
the Discipleship Ministry Team at faithoutloud@cumberland.org

OUR UNITED OUTREACH
Made Possible In Part By Your Tithe To Our United Outreach

Table of Contents

Curriculum Users Guide. v

Lesson 1: Cleanliness 1

Lesson 2: Visions: Are You Crazy? 7

Lesson 3: Listen to God and Clean Up Your Mess! 15

Lesson 4: Stubborn Kids: Beware! 23

Lesson 5: Happy Vengeance: Does God Endorse Baby Killing? 31

Lesson 6: Monsters in the Bible 41

Lesson 7: Eat What? Drink What? 53

Lesson 8: Social Stoning: Are You Without Sin? 63

Lesson 9: Weird Deaths in the Bible 69

Lesson 10: Curses in the Bible 80

Lesson 11: Weird Sexual References in the Bible 91

Lesson 12: That's Not in the Bible?!? 105

Lesson 13: Common Sayings That Come from the Bible 119

Welcome to the Faith Out Loud curriculum!

It is our prayer that these lessons both encourage you and equip you as a youth leader—we're so grateful for what you do in the lives of students!

Blessings to you and your ministry!

Below are explanations of the components found in each lesson and tips for using this curriculum.

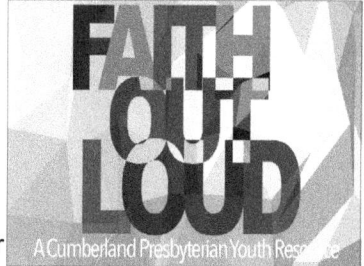

Lesson Title: Each lesson has a catchy title. Use these titles as teasers to get your students excited about upcoming gatherings.

Scripture: Each lesson has a key scripture reference. Spend some time studying and praying through each week's passage as you prepare to teach.

Theme: The theme statement gives you a quick snapshot into the main point of the lesson.

Leader Prep: This section is usually divided into two parts: Resource List and Leader Prep. Resource List give you a quick list of all the stuff you need to gather for each week. Leader Prep give detailed instructions on the advance work that needs to be done for that week's activities. Do NOT wait until the night before you teach to review this section.

The Lesson: Once you move into the teaching time, you'll see these recurring elements:

- ✓ **Get Started:** These activities are designed to draw students into the material and set up the theme for the lesson.

- ✓ **Discussion Questions:** Usually a group of open-ended questions, these moments in the lesson are strategically placed to encourage your students to both think about and respond to the topic at hand.

- ✓ **Say:** Placed in italics, these sections can be read verbatim to your students to help them fully understand the implications of the topic or theme. You'll discover you'll get the best response when you are thoroughly familiar with these sections and can deliver the same information in your own words instead of just reading the info to the students.

- ✓ **Leader Tips:** You'll find sections of side notes throughout each lesson. These are notes just for you, the leader. These notes offer you everything from instructions on how to facilitate the activities to background information on the subject to tips for making your lesson run smoothly.

- ✓ **Listen Up:** This section highlights a key scripture passage that should be read aloud. Encourage student to do these readings as often as possible.

- ✓ **Now What:** This section helps your students respond to the lesson. This will drive the lesson home and get your students thinking about the lesson in terms outside of the classroom walls.

- ✓ **Live It:** This is simply just the closing of each lesson, designed to help you conclude your time with your students well and offer them something to think about in the week ahead. Most weeks have handouts to pass along to your students during this time. You may find it helpful to encourage your students to get a folder to keep these handouts together so they can easily refer to them during the week.

- ✓ **Handouts:** At the end of some lessons, you'll find a reproducible page. Your purchase of this curriculum grants you the right to print and distribute copies to everyone in your group.

- ✓ **Just in Case/Digging Deeper:** These provide opportunities to continue the lesson and enable further learning.

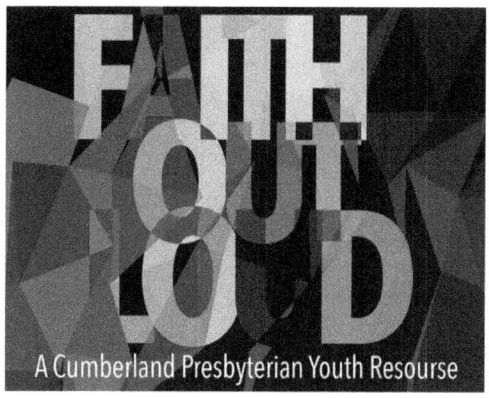

Cleanliness
by Melissa Reid Goodloe

Scripture: Psalm 51:10

Theme: The cleanliness that God requires is much more than taking a bath. God wants to clean us from the inside out.

Resource List

- Markers, crayons, colored pencils
- 3 sheets of newsprint for questions
- Sheet of newsprint for each group
- Index cards
- Tape
- Pens/pencils
- Bibles
- Flower bulbs/potted tree
- Tools to plant flowers/tree

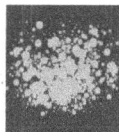

Leader Prep

- Read the scripture. With only one verse, the Psalmist cries out to God for a cleanliness that we hopefully all desire: to be Christ-like.

Label Newsprint:
 #1 What does it mean to be clean?
 #2 How do we wash our insides?
 #3 What is a right spirit?

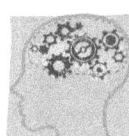

Leader Insight

Connecting to Your Students
Most people wish to be clean. We shower daily, wash our clothes, and practice good hygiene, yet we constantly put harmful things into our bodies, let dirty words escape our mouths, and make filthy choices. It is easy for some people to justify putting things that are unhealthy for us in our mouths. It is easy to laugh off an uncomfortable scene in a movie. It is easy to say that those bad words went in one ear and out the other. God desires us to be Christ-like. Would you offer God something unhealthy? Would you take God to see that movie? Would you say curse words or listen to others speak foully with God standing there? Most of us would answer "no," but the thing is, God is there! This is the

Notes:

message that everyone—youth and all—desperately needs to hear. It is *OK* if you slip up, but slipping up doesn't constitute diving in head-first and immersing one's self intentionally.

Explaining the Bible

Martin Luther is quoted as saying that the Psalms are "a little Bible." The title comes from the Septuagint, a translation of the Hebrew Bible in Greek, and it refers to stringed instruments. The original title came from a word meaning "praises." The psalms are a collection of prayers, praises, and laments—many written by or for King David. For thousands of years people have memorized, sung, and prayed these Hebrew poems. These psalms were compiled over several centuries and were most likely completed in the third century B.C.

Psalm 51 is grouped with six other psalms (Ps. 6, 32, 38, 102, 130, and 143) to make what is known as the seven penitential (relating to or expressing repentence) psalms. These are normally grouped and said together during the time of Lent. Many psalms have what is called superscriptions that help us locate and understand a particular psalm. Psalm 51's superscription tells us that this is a psalm of David written as a result of the situation between David, the prophet Nathan, and Bathsheba. You can read this story in 2 Samuel 11-12:25.

The prophet Nathan comes to David after David has called the married Bathsheba to the palace to sleep with her. David knows that he has sinned and that he is not right with God. David comes to God and cries out. He knows that he has a problem and only God can fix it. David seeks God's forgiveness. He wants to be made clean. He does not wish for his relationship with God to be broken. He asks God not only to cleanse him, but to cleanse him from the inside out. He asks God to do what we cannot. A man can wash away the dirt on the outside and choose not to dirty up the inside anymore, but only God has the power to renew and restore a right spirit. Only God has the power of forgiveness that takes away the sin and leaves us filled with peace and joy.

Theological Underpinnings

In 2 Samuel we find David and Bathsheba. David commits adultery with Bathsheba, which he knows is a sin. David's fear is that the Lord will be angry with him and depart from him as he had from Saul. In this psalm, David seeks pardon, confesses his sins to God, asks for forgiveness, seeks to be made clean, commits to service, and prays for his country.

This psalm is a good example of repentance, and it should be used whether it is prayed, spoken, or sung when seeking God's forgiveness. The desire to have a clean heart and right spirit should not belong only to David, but to all Christians.

Applying the Lesson to Your Own Life
What does it mean to be Christ-like? Take a moment to write down the qualities that Christ possesses. Now put a check next to the qualities that you share with Christ. Are there qualities you need to work harder to achieve? Are there things that you feel are not within your reach? Christ is our example, and we are the examples for the youth that we teach. Do you possess a clean heart? Is there a right spirit inside of you? Lift up a prayer to God to make you a Christ-like example.

Notes:

Leader Tip:
You will use your list of qualities that Christ possesses as an example for students to look at as they make their own list.

The Lesson

Get Started (10 min.)

Say: **Today we are talking about cleanliness. Then ask your students to list out loud all the things they do to get clean (shower, bath, washing your face, brushing your teeth, washing clothes, etc.).**

Then say, **When you look in a mirror, are you clean? When God sees what is on your inside, are you clean?**

List on newsprint the following questions:

- What does it mean to be clean?
- How do we wash our insides?
- What is a right spirit?

Have students write their answers to the questions on the newsprint and then pair up. Once paired, have them compare their answers with one another. Then ask each pair to share at least one of their answers with the entire group.

Notes:

Leader Tip:
If you have no real experience or knowledge on how to plant flowers or trees you might want to see if there is someone in your church who would partner with you to help you do this part of the lesson. You might want to send a message to your youth and parents that you are planning an outdoor activity and they might be getting dirty. You can also read this link that will help explain a bit more about what it might take to plant something at your church. http://www.lowes.com/cd_planting+trees+and+shrubs_440897451_

Listen Up (15 min.)

Choose one of the following two activites:

- Read the scripture and break into small groups. Give each group a piece of newsprint, and ask them to draw a picture that represents this scripture. Be sure to have plenty of markers, sharpies, crayons, or colored pencils available.

After each group has drawn their picture, have each small group share their picture with the whole class and discuss why they drew what they drew.

- Go outside to preplanned area where you will plant some flowers and/or tree. Read the scripture. Explain that David was asking God to create in him a new heart. That David wanted God to plant a new and right spirit within him.

Then say, **David knew that he needed more than just forgiveness. David needed a clean heart and a new, right spirit. David knew he could not be the servant, the King, the child of God he wanted to be and remain the same person.**

Tell students that planting flowers/trees is much like God creating a new heart, a new spirit within us. God must prepare our hearts just as we have to prepare the soil. He must dig up and around the soil to create space to plant something new. These flowers/trees we are planting will be a reminder of God's desire to create in us a new heart and put a right spirit within us.

As you are planting, ask the students, **In what areas in your life do you need a new heart and a new spirit?**

Share some of your thoughts on these things with your students to keep them focused on lesson as you are planting flowers/trees.

Now What? (15 min.)

Say: **What does it mean to be Christ-like? I want you to take a moment to write down the qualities that Christ possesses.**

After giving students a few moments, say; **Now put a check next to the qualities that you share with Christ. Are there qualities you need to work harder to achieve? Are there things that you feel are not within your reach?**

Allow students to discuss their answers before moving on to next part of the lesson.

Live It (5 min.)

Have students break up into pairs, and have them share with one another what they would like to give up. If they are not comfortable with sharing, just asking them to tell their partner to pray for them. After each pair shares and prays, ask them to stand up and hold hands while praying the prayer of David.

The Prayer of David

**Dear God,
Create in me a clean heart and put a new and right spirit within me. Amen.**

Resources used: http://www.lowes.com/cd_planting+trees+and+shrubs_440897451_, Bible Gateway

© 2015 Discipleship Ministry Team of the Ministry Council of the Cumberland Presbyterian Church. All Rights Reserved.

Notes:

Leader Tip:
If you chose the outdoor activity you can discuss these questions with your group as you are planting or after you are done. Use the list you made during *applying the lesson to your own life* to help you lead the discussion.

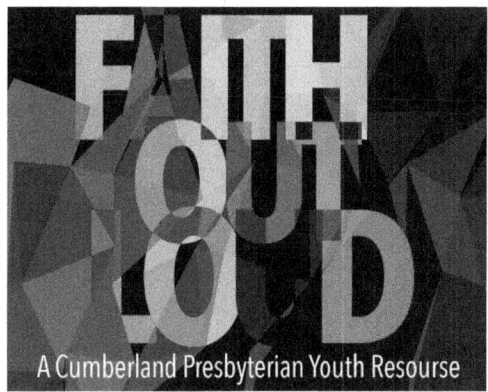

Visions: Are You Crazy?
by Melissa Reid Goodloe

Scripture: Acts 2:17

Theme: God is still using visions and dreams to reveal God's plan. God seeks to speak with us, though we can be closed off spiritually, mentally, and physically.

Resource List

- Markers
- 3 sheets of newsprint
- Tape
- Pens/pencils
- Bibles
- Poster board
- Magazines/picture books
- Scissors

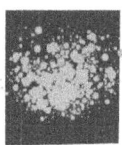

Leader Prep

- Read the scriptures. Study the specific examples of visions or dreams.
- Gen. 28:12-13 (Jacob); 2 Sam. 7:17 (Nathan); Daniel 8:1-3, 15-27 (Daniel); Daniel 5: 5-19 (Daniel); Luke 24:22-23 (women at the tomb); Acts 9:10 (Ananias); Acts 10:10-20 (Peter); Acts 16:9 (Paul); Revelation 4:2 (John)
- Label newsprint:
    #1 What do you dream about at night?
    #2 Name some people to whom God revealed things through visions and dreams?
    #3 Do you believe God can still reveal things today through visions/dreams?

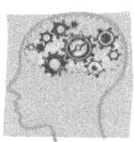

Leader Insight

Connecting to Your Students
Merriam Webster defines vision as: something that you imagine: a picture that you see in your mind; Something that you see or dream especially as part of a religious or supernatural experience.

Notes:

Some youth may have experienced visions or dreams they cannot explain. Some may have experienced déjà vu or felt the need to complete a task once they awoke. Some may feel that they will be made fun of if they talk about these things. Some may feel that the idea of visions is ludicrous and silly.

It is important to creating a safe environment where youth feel comfortable—a place to share and discuss, a place where respect is key, a place where everyone's thoughts and feelings are valued.

Explaining the Bible

The Acts of the Apostles contains the stories of the early church. Not simply a history book, Acts helps readers enter into the lives and practices of the earliest followers of Jesus as well as showing what the early church looked like.

Most scholars believe that the Gospel of Luke and Acts were both written by Luke. Luke was a doctor and a trusted friend and helper of Paul. The book of Acts is addressed to Theophilus, a name meaning "dear to God."

It is unknown if Theophilus is a historical figure or a metaphor. Scholars have stated that this book might have been used as catechism for the early followers of Christ and that Theophilus was a young convert to this new faith. The book itself was most likely written between 70-100 A.D.

Luke wrote Acts by compiling the testimonies from apostles and leaders in the early church along with his own personal witness of events. William Willimon, from the Interpretation Bible Commentary Series, says that the Acts of the Apostles reads like a "travel diary of the early church."

Our story today comes from one of the most famous passages of Acts: the event at Pentecost.

This piece of scripture was originally found in the Old Testament, Joel 2:28. The scripture prophesies about the last days or day of the Lord. This is a time when the Holy Spirit will be poured out upon the people.

This lesson's scripture from the book of Acts follows the outpouring of the Holy Spirit at Pentecost. Peter is explaining to the people what has just taken place. They are not drunk but filled with the Holy Spirit just as Joel prophesied.

This is the beginning of the fulfillment of this prophecy. We live in the end times. No one knows when Christ will return, but we should be prepared. The scripture talks of old and young, male and female joined together by the Holy Spirit for one purpose. That purpose is to spread the gospel. This is not an obscure passage about something taking place in ancient times; this is taking place even now!

Theological Underpinnings

End times, or last days, was a term commonly used in the Old Testament, meaning a time when the Messiah would set up his kingdom. Peter uses the scripture from Joel to explain the events that have taken place; a multitude of people heard his message being spoken in their own language. This occurred due to the outpouring of the Holy Spirit. Through our baptism, the Holy Spirit is poured out upon each believer. We need to be open spiritually, mentally, and physically to hear God, to block out distraction, and to avoid obstacles that keep us from following God's will.

Applying the Lesson to Your Own Life

Each day we seem to get busier and busier. We constantly say "yes" when we should say "no." We do not take time out for quiet times with God. Often we do not even allow for enough sleep. God spoke to all kinds of people in visions and dreams. Why would we think that God just stopped? We are not open to God mentally, physically, or spiritually. We are closed off, and if we do hear from God, we don't want people to think we're crazy. Take time as you prepare this lesson to open up to God. Take a quiet moment during the day to simply open your mind to God. Read scripture or a favorite verse before you fall asleep at night. Take some much needed time and relax. Remember, even if God screamed at us, it would be impossible to hear if we are tuned out during the day.

Notes:

Notes:

Leader Tip:

Theme scripture is Acts 2:17

The Lesson

Get Started (10 min.)

Today we are talking about visions. Visions are not usually something we talk about. Many people today would dismiss speaking of visions as someone running a scam or someone delusional. However, God uses visions as a way to communicate many different things. God still use visions today if we are open to receive them.

Direct your students' attention to the questions on the newsprint:

- What do you dream about at night?
- Name some people to whom God revealed things through visions and dreams?
- Do you believe God can still reveal things today through visions/dreams?

Have the students go around and write their answers on the sheets with markers. Feel free to discuss the answers afterward.

Listen Up (15 min.)

Read the theme scripture and then break into small groups.

Say: **According to dictionary.com a vision is:**

1. the act or power of sensing with the eyes; sight.

2. the act or power of anticipating that which will or may come to be: prophetic vision; the vision of an entrepreneur.

3. an experience in which a personage, thing, or event appears vividly or credibly to the mind, although not actually present, often under the influence of a divine or other agency: a heavenly messenger appearing in a vision.

4. something seen or otherwise perceived during such an experience: The vision revealed its message.

5. a vivid, imaginative conception or anticipation: visions of wealth and glory.

6. something seen; an object of sight.

7. a scene, person, etc., of extraordinary beauty: The sky was a vision of red and pink.

After sharing the definitions, share a time when you might have had a vision. It can be serious or funny but give students a chance to hear from you as the leader. After sharing your story, give each small group one of the specific vision scriptures to look at.

Discussion Questions:

- How did the person in your story react to their vision?
- What did he or she see?
- What was the message?

After a few minutes to read and discuss, have each group share with the entire group.

Say: **There are many books on the subject of visions and dreams. Some of those books even contain a guide on what an object or scenerio in someone's vision or dream could mean. In scripture, most of the visions have a clear understood message. In the passages we just read each vision or dream had a particular purpose and message that God wanted to communicate.**

Notes:

Leader Tip:
If you don't feel comfortable sharing your own story invite your pastor or another leader from your church to share.

Leader Tip:
Many of the visions and dreams in the Bible speak about the situations and circumstances during the times they were living. It's passe to consider these texts without considering their cultural context. Your students may have heard these texts explained differently. Try to help them see these texts within their specific context.

Notes:

Take some time and share the following with your students.

Gen. 28:12-13 (Jacob)
God promises Jacob a home and promises to be faithful.

2 Sam. 7:17 (Nathan)
He hears God and speaks that message to King David.

Daniel 5:5-19, 8:1-3, 15-27 (Daniel)
God speaking about the end of an age, or the coming end of the ruling powers.

Luke 24:22-23 (women at the tomb)
Angels who told the women Jesus is alive.

Acts 9:10 (Ananias)
God uses a vision to send Ananias to look for Saul.

Acts 10:10-20 (Peter)
God uses a trance to help Peter show hospitality.

Acts 16:9 (Paul)
God speaks through a vision to Paul to go to Macedonia.

Revelation 4:2 (John)
John is shown a whole series of visions to help encouage followers of Jesus during persecution.

After shairing, ask students if they have ever had a vision/dream like these from God? What did they do afterwards?

Now What? (15 min.)

Make a Vision Board

Before the lesson put up a poster board or newsprint on the wall. Try to put it in a place where it can stay permanently or where you can easily take it down and put it elsewhere. The idea is to keep it so it's a visualzation for your students every time they meet.

Say: **We are going to make a vision board. The idea is to create something that looks like a collage that represents the vision God has for our group. We spend lots of time talking about what God wants for us and what God wants us to do, but God wants us to have a vision for our group. We are going to take some time and use pictures and words to create a vision board. Before we begin let's take a minute to pray for vision.** Say a quick prayer.

After praying, say: **Now we are going to create our vision board. Use the magazines and Bibles to cut out or write down an answer to the questions I'm about to read and put them on our vision board.**

Read your group the questions and let them begin.

Discussion Questions:

- What is your favorite scripture? Write it out and put it on the board.
- How could we help others as a group? Find a picture or words to describe how and put it on the board.
- Where is God in our world? Find a picture or words to describe where and put it on the board.

After they are done, clean up the space and if you haven't already done so, put the board or newsprint on the wall.

 ## Live It (5 min.)

Say: **Take a picture of the vision board with your cell phone. Every morning this week look at it and think about our groups' vision.**

Say this prayer or one similar to it: **Dear God, help us to be open to hear your voice and see your visions. Amen.**

Resources used: NIV Bible Study Commentary by John H. Sailhamer, Bible Gateway

© 2015 Discipleship Ministry Team of the Ministry Council of the Cumberland Presbyterian Church. All Rights Reserved.

Notes:

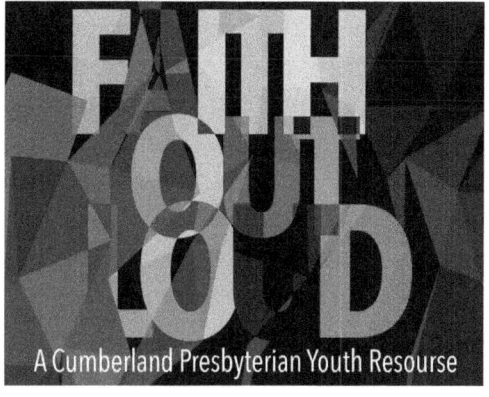

Listen To God And Clean Up Your Mess!
by Melissa Reid Goodloe

Scripture: Deuteronomy 23:12-14 and Malachi 2:2-3

Theme: God desires for us to listen to the commands God gives. When we do not listen, things get messy.

Resource List

- Newsprint
- Markers
- Pens
- drop cloth/tarp
- long table
- Food item (cereal, spagetti, ice cream)
- Apron or bib
- blindfold/bandanas
- towels
- water
- index cards

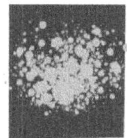

Leader Prep

- Read the scriptures and familiarize yourself with other excrement verses (Isaiah 36:12, Ezekiel 4:12-15)

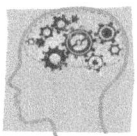

Leader Insight

Connecting to Your Students
Excrement can be a funny subject depending on the age group with which you work (though some will definitely find it funny at any age). Some students may have a hard time getting past the silly aspects of the subject matter and will struggle to focus on what God has to say in the scriptures. You might have to reign in the conversation if it gets out of hand. Also remember you might have some that are embarrassed by the topic or feel uncomfortable with the discussion.

Explaining the Topic
Deuteronomy is a book about identity formation. It speaks to a people who are not yet a nation. The Hebrew people are on the cusp of entering in to their long ago promised land. Led by their once reluctant leader, Moses, Deuteronomy is an amalgamation of the other books of Moses. Though the origin and date of Deuteronomy is increasingly believed to be much later than the time period it speaks to, many of the teachings within the book are consistent with the time.

Notes:

The name Deuteronomy is taken from a passage from the Greek Septuagint, meaning "second law." As many scholars point out this is really a misinformed title, but it has stuck through the centuries. The Hebrew title translates into "words." The book of Deuteronomy is directly or indirectly (depending on which historian you read) the "words" of Moses. The book is loosely broken into three long speeches concerning Israel's history, the law, and covenant with God.

A majority of the book is an explanation of the Law of Moses, not just a copy of it. It explains to a growing group of people the way to live in their new land. A people who spent 40 years in the wilderness trying to rid themselves of a destructive identity formed in the grips of slavery are now given these "words" to form a new identity.

The passage for the lesson is in a group of passages dealing with purity for the community during times of war. These instructions from God make perfect sense to anyone who has ever gone camping. You build your toilet area outside of the camp. You bring a tool, as suggested, either a trowel or a shovel, and you dig a hole. Then you clean up your mess by covering up your excrement. No one, the Lord included, wants to walk through your campsite and worry about seeing anything indecent.

The book of Malachi is the last book in what we call the Old Testament. Malachi is the last of the Minor Prophets (Hosea, Joel, Amos, Obadiah, Jonah, Micah, Nahum, Habakkuk, Zephaniah, Haggai, Zechariah, and Malachi) in Israel's history.

The word Malachi means "my messenger," and it is not known whether this was the title or proper name of the prophet. The world of Malachi is much different than that of many of the other prophets. As most of the prophets spoke of the hope of God to rescue the people and rebuild the Temple, Malachi was recorded during a time when the people were no longer in exile and the Temple had been rebuilt. Malachi faced a much different challenge than many of prophets before him.

Many times prophets spoke to people who were being abused and misused; Malachi spoke to a generation who had lost touch with the trials they once faced. They were indifferent to the past generations' love of God and were slipping deeper into a slow fade of indifference towards the God of Israel.

Malachi's prophetic message was to wake up the people to their need to obey God with passion and to critique the priests who God felt were contributing to the people's lukewarm faith.

Malachi's verse is pretty straightforward. You can listen to my commands, or I will put you out of my presence. If only the verse was that simple. Then God goes and spreads dung on their faces. Not just any dung but the dung of the animal they presented as an offering. This is like a double slap to the face.

Theological Underpinnings
There are several verses that refer to excrement and dung in the Bible. One refers to the people of the city who sit on the wall where Isaiah is talking to the leaders. Isaiah says that if they continue to follow the wrong leaders, they will end up eating their own dung and drinking urine. In Ezekiel, we encounter bread being prepared to eat by baking it over human dung. If you have never defiled yourself, the Lord might allow you to cook with cow dung instead.

The passage in Deuteronomy is in line with a whole host of passages dealing with purity. The instruction to dig a hole and cover your business is a practical instruction to keep thousands of people healthy in the wild. Our Malachi passage is a harsh warning to the priestly class. It's a humiliating and embarrassing gesture to match their humiliating and embarrassing way of representing God.

Applying the Lesson to Your Own Life
Were you ever a boy or girl scout? If not, have you ever been camping? Think about the rules for a clean campsite, for having clean water, and how best not to contaminate either. The world contaminates us on a daily basis, bombarding us with temptations. Many times we find ourselves in a mess. Most often that mess could have been avoided if we had just listened to God and followed the commandments set before us.

No one wants dung spread over his or her face, yet sometimes we wake up just covered in mess. Think about the way you listen to God—are you really listening and trying to hear that still, small voice? When you make a mess, do you clean it up or leave it for someone else to worry about or worse, leave it for someone else to step in it?

Notes:

Notes:

Leader Tip:
If you have a large group just select a few of the students and allow the others to watch. You might want to choose volunteers in advance so they can have a change of clothing just in case.

The Lesson

Get Started (15 min.)

Say: **Today's lesson is about messes. When we do not listen to God, we end up in a whole lot of mess.**

Choose one of the following two activities:

- **Discussion Questions**

Welcome students to go around the room and answer the questions listed on the newsprint.

List on newsprint the following:
- Name one thing you do to prepare your campsite when camping.
- What is the best way to listen to God?
- What should God do when people don't listen?

Spend some time talking to the stdents about their answers. Ask them what they wrote down and why. After a number of students respond move on into next section.

- **Make A Mess**

Before this activity make sure to set up the room. You might want to get a drop cloth or tarp to cover the floor. Set up a table with chairs and have a few aprons or bibs along with some water and towels to clean up after the activity.

During this activity students will form pairs. One will be the "hands" while the other gives instructions on what to do. Have one person sit down around the table and put their hands behind their backs.

Have the other person sit or stand behind them and place their arms to where now their arms will replace the person's sitting down arms and then have them put on a blindfold.

Once they get settled tell them they are going to prepare a meal. The "arms" must listen to the person sitting at the table as they will not be able to see. The person who is able to prepare the meal with the least amount of mess is the winner.

After students have completed the activity and get settled back into the room, say:

It's easy to make a mess of things. Today we are going to explore two passages of scripture that are not usually read in church. Both scriptures talk about excrement. We are going to read both of these passages aloud and then do an activity. No, it's not what you think.

 ## Listen Up (20 min.)

Ask the students to read both scriptures.

Ask: **Why do you think these passages are in the Bible?**

After students respond, take some time and summarize the "Explaining the Bible" and "Theological Underpinnings" sections. Once you have explained a bit of the context of each passage, say: **Now we are going to break into two groups and create a skit based on both scriptures.**

Have the students break into groups.

Give them multiple Bibles with different translations of the text they will be creating a skit with. This may allow them to get a better feel for the scripture to help them better act it out.

Give students about 10 minutes to come up with their skit. Have each group share their skit with the group. Once they are finished move on in the lesson.

Notes:

Leader Tip:
HEADS UP! More than likely this will be silly and might be on the edge of what you deem appropriate. Another activity would be to print off copies of "Explaining the Bible" and "Theoligical Underpinnings" for each student and read and discuss.

Notes:

Now What? (15 min.)

"How Well Do You Know Your Neighbor, Or Something Stinks"?

Pass out index cards, one per person. Have them choose a partner, but not their best friend or someone they know well. One partner answers 5 questions about himself or herself.

Four of the answers will be the truth, and one answer is a lie.

Once both partners have answered the questions, they must take turns making introductions of their partner to the group by sharing the answers to their partner's questions.

The group has to decide what about that person "stinks," or is the lie.

Questions:
- What is your full name?
- Do you have siblings-brothers/sisters. If so, how many?
- Do you have pets? dogs/cats/other?
- Name one fact about yourself that most people don't know?
- What is your most embarrassing moment?

After a few people have gone, say: **The Bible teaches us that all scripture is God-breathed and useful. It takes time to get to know someone. In the same manner, it takes time, it takes years of listening and reading the Bible, to understand how passages like we read today can inspire, teach, and convict us.**

Just as we need to pay attention to details to know someone, we have to pay attention to the details of scripture to know its true intent.

If we just pluck some scripture out of the Bible with no context, it might be amusing but it's not as God intended us to study scripture.

Live It (5 min.)

Say: **Though these passages can be difficult to understand, it's important to study the whole Bible and not just skip over those parts that don't make sense. But this can take some time free of distractions.**

Form a circle and get everyone to hold hands.

Tell them that you are about to have a time of prayer. You will go around the circle where each person will have an opportunity to pray. If the person doesn't feel like praying they can just gently squeeze the hand of the person on their left. After everyone has had a chance to pray, finish the prayer and say Amen.

© 2015 Discipleship Ministry Team of the Ministry Council of the Cumberland Presbyterian Church. All Rights Reserved.

Notes:

Stubborn Kids: BEWARE!
by Melissa Goodloe

Scripture: Deuteronomy 21:18-21

Theme: We serve a God of multiple chances, but God desires our obedience.

Resource List

- Markers
- 4 sheets newsprint
- Tape
- Pens/pencils
- Paper
- Post-it notes or blank white labels
- Bibles
- You will need a way to show images from a website. You can either just have it on your laptop monitor or connect it to a projecter/screen.

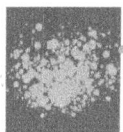

Leader Prep

- Read the scripture. Even though we talk about God's forgiveness and multiple chances, the law says stubborn kids should obey or be stoned!

- Label newsprint:

    #1 Is being stubborn or rebellious actual disobedience?

    #2 What is a fair punishment for disobedience?

    #3 If you knew you would be stoned for disobedience, would this change your actions or behaviors?

- Familiarize yourself with The Brick Testament. Prior to using this resource look at link on how to use Brick Testament at http://www.thebricktestament.com/churches/

Please follow instructions of copyright indicated on website. Brick Testament Lesson Link: http://www.thebricktestament.com/the_law/when_to_stone_your_children/dt21_18a.html

- Pray this prayer:

Dear God,

I want to follow your ways. Please help me to focus on what is pleasing to you. Please take away my stubbornness and help me to obey. Amen.

Notes:

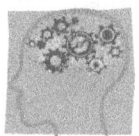

Leader Insight

Connecting to Your Students
Many youth get labeled (stubborn, weird, attitude problem, disruptive, manipulative), but God's only label is child! Youth group is a safe place for students to be themselves, and often the problems parents see in their youth are not seen by youth workers.

On the other hand, there will be those who act out in youth group to receive the attention they crave from loved ones. Rebellion comes in many forms. Some youth are seeking a relationship, and they will latch on to any form of attention, whether it is for positive or negative behavior. Remember to focus this lesson on obedience and positive reinforcement.

Explaining the Topic
The Hebrew people are on the edge of entering the Promised Land. They had traveled for years in the wilderness, becoming a people and nation, and now they will finally have a land to call home. A land needs order, and so Deuteronomy helps explain to the people how this new land would be governed. Much of the book explains the Decalogue, or Ten Commandments, found in Deuteronomy 5. All the rules and laws found in the chapters of Deuteronomy help to illuminate the Ten Commandments.

The fifth commandment, honor your father and mother, found in Exodus 20:12 and Deuteronomy 5:16, is inspiration for the passage in this lesson. It was fundamental to the harmony of the community for children to honor their parents. Deuteronomy 21:18-21 echoes another passage found in what scholars call the holiness code in Leviticus. That passage reads,

Anyone who curses their father or mother is to be put to death. Because they have cursed their father or mother, their blood will be on their own head. Lev. 20:9

The scripture is clear. The law is written that a stubborn or rebellious child who has been given opportunities for correction and obedience be taken to the elders. Then the elders are to stone him or her. But it's not that simple.

For one, we tend to think of stubborn and rebellious being things like back talking or staying out past curfew. This law wasn't speaking about that type of stubbornness or rebellion. Stubborn and rebellious weren't terms thrown around so lightly. The passage itself uses the words, "He is a glutton and a drunkard." This presents the case that this is not just a small offense but rather more like a complete, and most likely dangerous, offense.

Secondly, the elders acted as the ruling body of the people. The elders had the power to decide someone's fate based on the law they were chosen to uphold. So, it wasn't as simple as just having a kid smart off and you take them to be killed. This was most likely a law for the most extreme of rebellion.

God repeatedly tells us to obey our father and mother in Deuteronomy, The Ten Commandments, and Proverbs, to name just a few places. God desires this obedience from us. This creates order within our families.

This does not just apply to our earthly parents but to the parent we find in God as we become heirs. God desires us to honor our covenant. God does not take us out and stone us or even turn us away at the gate. God gives us multiple chances to restore a relationship. When we give up our stubbornness, our rebellion, and restore our covenant with God, only then will we find peace.

Theological Underpinnings
Most scholars do not believe that stoning was an acceptable form of punishment for children, even in the Old Testament. In fact, many point out that there are no recorded instances of this practice taking place. This seems like a harsh punishment, but it is a harsh example used to show the importance of mutual respect. Order was needed in the family as well as in society. Without order, there was chaos.

Notes:

Notes:

The rules set forth by the Pentateuch were to help believers grow closer to God by following closely to the commandments, regarding everything from diet to burnt offerings. With the coming of Jesus Christ, many of these laws were discontinued because the ritual was present but not the devotion and obedience to God was not.

Applying the Lesson to Your Own Life

Can you recall a time in your life when you would have been labeled stubborn or rebellious? What caused a change in you? Was it a program at church or within the community? Was it a special person who mentored or understood you? Think about the road you travelled to get to adulthood, and make a list of people and programs that helped you.

As you prepare for this lesson, think about the young people in your youth group. Who needs help? Who could you mentor? Who reminds you of yourself at that age? Who is struggling? Once you have answered these questions, think of ways to engage and help these young people the way you were helped along the way.

The Lesson

Get Started (10 min.)

Today's lesson is about stubborn kids. Ask students:

Would you consider yourself stubborn or rebellious? Would others have the same opinion?

List on newsprint the following:
- Is being stubborn or rebellious actual disobedience?
- What is a fair punishment for disobedience?
- If you knew you would be stoned, would this change your actions or behaviors?

Have the students write their answers on the newsprint. Feel free to discuss the answers however you see fit.

Listen Up (15 min.)

Choose one of the following two activites:

- **A Modern Tale**

Have youth break into smaller groups.

Once they have formed there groups have them open their Bibles and read Deuteronomy 21:18-21.

After they have read the passage, say: **Now you are going to make this a modern tale. In your groups, rewrite this passage of scripture. Rewrite it using a modern day scenirio.**

Make sure each group has pens and paper to write out their story.

Once groups are done writing their stories have them read them aloud to the rest of the groups.

- **The Brick Testament (see Leader Prep)**

Set up a computer or screen to share Brick Testament's version of Deuteronomy 21:18-21.

http://www.thebricktestament.com/the_law/when_to_stone_your_children/dt21_18a.html

Questions to ask group after each activity:
- What do you think stubborn and rebellious meant to the people back then?
- Is that similar to what we think of when we label someone stubborn and rebellious? How is it the same? How is it not the same?
- How are you punished when you are stubborn and/or rebellious?

Notes:

Leader Tip:
Just for fun have some people in the other groups act out the stories as they are being read aloud.

Notes:

Notes:

Share with your group some information from Explaining the Topic and Theological Underpinnings section.

Once you are done move to next section.

Now What? (15 min.)

Say the following: **Think about the times you struggle with obedience at school, with parents, during sports, following God. Now take the post-its or stickers, and write out a sentence to remind you obedience to others is obedience to God.**

Take these stickers with you and post them. Put them on your bathroom mirror, inside your locker, on your car's dashboard—anywhere you think you will see them and be reminded!

Example:
Today I will smile and say, "YES," when asked to clean my room.

Tonight I will read my Bible before I play games or text.

Give students some time to write there notes and ask if any of them would like to share what they wrote down and why.

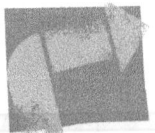

Live It (5 min.)

Choose a friend to help keep you accountable to your challenge and to pray for you this week. Take time to close together with a prayer.

Resources used: The Brick Testament, Bible Gateway

© 2015 Discipleship Ministry Team of the Ministry Council of the Cumberland Presbyterian Church. All Rights Reserved.

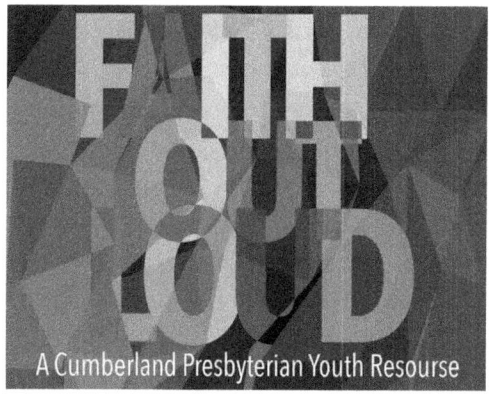

Happy Vengeance: Does God Endorse Baby Killing?
by T.J. Malinoski

Scripture: Psalm 137:9

Theme: Studying the Bible in various ways (comparing, listening, sharing) can help us understand difficult texts.

Resource List

- Copies of the Confession of Faith For Cumberland Presbyterians, for students to share
- New Revised Standard Version of the Bible
- Whiteboard or newsprint
- Writing utensils to be used on whiteboard and/or newsprint
- Copies of "4 Steps To Understanding God's Word" handout, enough for each student

Leader Prep

- Read over the scripture passage
- Have enough copies of the Confession of Faith For Cumberland Presbyterians for your youth
- Have enough copies of the New Revised Standard Version of the Bible for your youth
- Newsprint for "Pick & Choose" game with markers for each category
- Newsprint or whiteboard for the "Emotions List"
- Photocopy "4 Steps To Understanding God's Word" handout, enough for each student

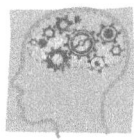

Leader Insight

Connecting to Your Students
The scriptures are full of biblical texts of words, names, places and meanings that are troubling to pronounce and difficult to understand. Be honest in sharing your own apprehensions when not knowing the exact pronunciation of word, the location of a place or the meaning of a particular verse. Youth may become frustrated in not knowing the meanings or sayings in the Bible. The lesson you are preparing may be the only time during the week that they come into contact with the scriptures.

Notes:

Digging Deeper:

The book of Psalms is a collection of songs—a hymnbook for the Hebrews to sing to God. The book of Psalms is often attributed to David, the same David who tended sheep as a boy, defeated Goliath, and became king to the Hebrews. A better translation from the Hebrew language to English is that many of the psalms are "for" David or "to" David, written in honor or memory of him. What sets Psalm 137 apart and makes it unique in comparison to all the other psalms is that it is written from the perspective of someone in captivity.

Leader Tip:

Jerusalem and Zion are used interchangeably to describe the same city.

Tell them of your resolve and the steps you take in lesson preparation and what you do when you become frustrated in your study of the scripture.

Explaining the Topic

Psalm 137:9 is the focus of our lesson. Verse nine closes the psalm with an appeal of happiness that could come from taking "little ones" and dashing them against the rocks. Isolating the verse, we find a twisted desire to do bodily harm, with the intent of death, to infants and small children. The natural response to such a verse is repulsion and to classify the text as a mistranslation. Biblical commentators and ministers alike avoid its meaning and rush on to uplifting themes of thanksgiving and praise found in the very next psalm. However, ignoring verse nine allows the text to be taken out of context. A verse that encourages such delight in hurting someone else, especially infants, is extremely troubling. What could be going on for the psalmist to make such a statement?

The writer of Psalm 137 is traveling and finds himself/herself along the banks of rivers of Babylon. A Hebrew in Babylon is a Hebrew in captivity. The two groups of people had been warring against one another for years. There was a sense of security that Hebrews felt during wartime because the walls of Jerusalem were constructed in such a way that penetration was difficult and served as a general discouragement against its enemies.

Over the years, the Hebrews were convinced that the walls of Jerusalem were impossible to overcome, deflecting enemy after enemy, raider after raider. But difficult and impossible are two different things. A people called the Edomites accepted the Jerusalem challenge, scaled the walls, and captured the coveted prize: the city of Jerusalem and its inhabitants.

Edomites are often described as a nomadic people, raiding villages and cities, then selling and trading their spoils of war to the highest bidder. Babylon, the nation-state in which the Edomites roamed, may very well have employed them in the difficult task of tearing down the walls. In the Edomite victory, Hebrew people are taken as captives and the psalm picks up their journey along the riverbanks enroute to the capital city of Chaldea. Stopping for a rest along the river, the writer and his people sit down and begin to weep, remembering their city of Zion.

The writer indicates that he is a musician, among other musicians, hanging their instruments in the nearby trees as they make camp. His future has most likely been determined. He will be an entertainer for his enemy until, that is, his enemy tires of his musical talents. Their captors command a song and in cruel humor, their tormentors want to hear a song from their destroyed city they left behind. The writer of the psalm then gives us a glimpse of his inner thoughts. Picture a man or woman exhausted from months of traveling, garnering what physical strength is left to push himself up. We can hear his inner anguish as he reaches for his instrument. "How can we sing God's songs while being deported?" We can feel his grief in the promise to render his right hand useless, his dominant hand, his playing hand, and to stifle his singing voice "If I ever forget you, O Jerusalem."

Then his thoughts take on a tone of an appeal. The misery, anguish, pain, and grief manifests in the most human form—an appeal for God to remember the day of Jerusalem's fall. Remember the chants of Edomites screaming, "Tear it down! Tear it down to its foundations!"

Lastly, we can hear the indictment: a fury of exasperation pouring out of someone full of bitterness and tired of humiliation, possibly spoken aloud, toward the Edomites, the daughters of Babylon, the plunderers, the captors, the tormentors and the devastators of the Hebrews. "Happy shall they be who pay you back what you have done to us! Happy shall they be who take your little ones and dash them against the rock!"

Theological Underpinnings

By itself, verse nine is a difficult text to digest and accept as even being scriptural. Knowing a little of its context and historical background gives meaning to the harsh language. It is not a question of acceptance or a pronouncement of how to treat infants and small children, but rather an exercise of attempting to understand the personal experience of the one who wrote Psalm 137.

The writer is speaking from a hopeless point of view. If his recent past and present circumstances are indicators of his near future, then his death is imminent. In a matter of weeks, life as a respected citizen with musical talents has been diminished to an entertainment for his captors.

Notes:

Notes:

He has become less than human, left only with memories and little hope. In his appeal in verses four through seven, we can read of his struggle of what appears to him to be the absence of God. Studying the text in this way, verse nine then can be understood as a desire, a wish, perhaps even a curse from a person in a powerless, hopeless position.

Applying the Lesson to Your Own Life
The author of this lesson has found this particular verse to be dark and depressing. How does one create a lesson for youth around a verse plucked out of context, and in studying the circumstances around the verse finds no additional help? While initially thinking that this may be a lesson about faithfulness or resistance (as it could possibly be written in such a way), it doesn't seem to do justice to psalmist's circumstances. The lesson focus is about what to do with such a difficult text when we have been taught to understand the scriptures as an authoritative guide and infallible rule for faith and practice on how to live a Christian life. Not every verse, collection of verses, or whole chapters in the scriptures can be used in this way. Therefore, applying this particular lesson to our own lives and to our youth's lives is to explore and expand how we approach God's inspired Word.

The Lesson

Get Started (10 min.)

"Pick And Choose"

Before your youth arrive, hang newsprint throughout the room for the seven categories listed: favorite color, favorite food, favorite movie, favorite band/singer, favorite brand of clothing, favorite bible verse. Feel free to alter the different "favorites" to reflect your group, but keep the favorite bible verse for this lesson. Under each category, list various choices (2 or more) of colors, movies, bands, clothing, and verses for your youth to choose from.

Begin by giving your youth five minutes to visit each category and to choose their favorite in each one. When the five minutes expires, ask the following questions:

What influenced your choice of color, food, band, movie, brand of clothing, and verse in the bible?
- Is it okay to pick and choose what verses of scripture we believe?
- Is it okay to pick and choose what verses of the scripture we are going to practice?

Listen Up (15 min.)

Give each youth copies of Psalm 137 (New Revised Standard Version), or have them find it in the Bible.

Say, **Psalm 137 is unique to all the other psalms. In just nine verses, it takes the reader back into time, moves into the present circumstances of the psalmist, and then describes what he/she wants the future to look like. The psalmist does this in just 155 words.**

Pay close attention to verse nine, which is the focal point of the lesson.

Then ask for volunteers or choose individuals to read the chapter.

Discussion Questions:

- What has happened to the writer of the psalm?
- What is the psalmist asked to do? By whom?
- What has the psalmist vowed to do if he/she forgets Jerusalem?
- What does the psalmist want to happen to his/her captors and tormentors?

Notes:

Notes:

Emotions List

Use the whiteboard or newsprint to list the emotions the psalmist may have felt or expressed in the Biblical text. To help your youth, look for words such as anger, anguish, bitterness, grief, homesick, humiliation, pain, miserable, pain, retaliation, retribution, resistance, sadness, suffering, tormented, vengeance.

Discussion Questions:

- How would you justify the psalmist's idea of payback? Can you?
- If you could speak with the psalmist, what would you say to the person who wrote this?

Following the discussion questions, read all of, or excerpts from, "Explaining The Bible" to your youth to provide insight and context for verse nine.

Now What? (25 min.)

"What Does Our Confession of Faith Say?"

Say: **Cumberland Presbyterians study and use the Confession of Faith to help articulate our understanding of what God has done and is doing in our world. The opening heading of the Confession of Faith is entitled "God Speaks To The Human Family." One way God speaks to us is in and through the scriptures.**

Distribute copies of the Confession of Faith to your youth. Have them read 1.05 under the heading, "The Holy Scriptures."

Discussion Questions:

- What does the Confession of Faith say about who writes the scriptures?
- What does the word "inspired" mean?
- What does the Confession of Faith say the scriptures are?
- How does the belief in the scriptures as "the infallible rule of faith and practice, the authoritative guide for Christian living" apply to Psalm 137:9?
- How should Cumberland Presbyterians interpret Psalm 137:9?

Say: **We believe that the scriptures are the infallible rule of faith and practice, the authoritative guide for Christian living. However, being happy at the destruction of "little ones" conflicts with the teachings of Jesus. For example, Jesus' teachings in Matthew 10 and 18 elevate the importance of infants and small children, while encouraging his followers to care for them and be more like them.**

Have your youth read Matthew 10:42; 18:6,10,14.

Discussion Questions:

- What does Jesus say about the treatment of "little ones"?
- How do we reconcile Psalm 137:9 in comparison to what Jesus says?

4 Steps To Understanding God's Word
Say: **Cumberland Presbyterians follow four steps in understanding God's word. We use these four steps to help determine how the scriptures are the infallible rule for faith and practice and the authoritative guide for Christian living.**

Distribute copies of the "4 Steps To Understanding God's Word" handout to each youth. Have your youth read 1.07 in the Confession of Faith and then complete the handout.

Notes:

Answer key:
1. Study "the writings of the Bible in their historical settings"
2. Compare "scripture with scripture"
3. Listen "to the witness of the church throughout the centuries"
4. Share "insights with others in the covenant community"

 ## Live It (5 min.)

Have your youth reread Psalm 137 in light of what they have learned. Ask for comments if their perception, opinion, or understanding of verse nine has changed and in what way.

Challenge your youth to put these four steps into practice in their personal Bible study, Sunday school class, and future meetings. If available, allow your youth to have their own copy of the Confession of Faith for reference and guidance.

Following closing comments and questions, close the lesson with the following prayer: **Most gracious God, your words inspire us, challenge us, and sometimes confuse us. Illuminate us with your own Spirit to help us understand your word in and through the scriptures. Be with us as we study the scriptures in their own setting. Help us compare the scriptures to one another. Open us to listen to your followers throughout the centuries. Encourage us to share our insights with others. Amen.**

© 2015 Discipleship Ministry Team of the Ministry Council of the Cumberland Presbyterian Church. All Rights Reserved.

4 Steps To Understanding God's Word

Complete the paragraph below from the Confession of Faith 1.07. As a challenge, see if you can fill-in the blanks without looking back at the text.

In order to understand God's word spoken in and through the scriptures, persons must have _____. Moreover, they should _____ the writings of the Bible in their historical settings, _____ scripture with scripture, _____ to the witness of the church throughout the centuries, and _____ insights with others in the covenant community.

The four steps to understanding God's Word are:
1.
2.
3.
4.

Monsters in the Bible
by Andy McClung

Scripture: Varied

Theme: Just like in our life, the Bible contains some mysteries we can figure out and some we can't.

Resource List

- Bibles of various translations, including King James Version
- Drawing paper and utensils
- Marker board/newsprint and markers
- (Optional) one six-sided die

Leader Prep

- In the week prior to this lesson, watch the news and/or scour the Internet for stories about new species being discovered, or scientists reversing their previous claims about something.

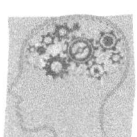

Leader Insight

Connecting to Your Students
Everybody loves a mystery. Many people are also quite curious about the weird, the unusual, and the not-easily-explained. Your students are no exception. Some of them may even be infatuated with so-called "reality" TV shows about ghost hunters or Bigfoot hunters. It may not have been long ago that some of them were really into the monsters within the literary worlds of Percy Jackson and Harry Potter, although they may find such things childish now.

Wondering about the unknown is not unhealthy. The fact that we can't fully know God (at least not in this life) makes God part of the unknown. It's important to note, however, that God is most definitely real. Dragons, unicorns, Bigfoot, and the Loch Ness Monster? Maybe they're real, and maybe they're not.

Notes:

Leader Tip:
Politically correct (adjective): agreeing with the idea that people should be careful not to use language or behave in a way that could offend a particular group of people.

There are lots of creatures mentioned in the Bible; some of them we could even call "monsters." That's what this lesson is about: monsters in the Bible. We won't cover supernatural beings, such as angels and fallen angels, or creatures seen in visions, or humans who acted monstrously.

Some of these monsters appear only in the King James Version (KJV) or earlier translations. Either later translators assumed these creatures never existed and therefore the previous translations must be wrong, or translation knowledge improved over the centuries.

Monster: **Behemoth**

Mentioned in: Job 40:15-24

Description: eats grass, strong legs and belly, has a tail, super strong bones, likes shade, is at home in the water, has eyes, has a nose that can pierce snares, has strong and thick tail

Possible Explanations: The Hebrew word for "beasts" sounds a lot like the English word "behemoth," and it's translated in most passages to mean animals or cattle. But Job 40 has a very specific description of a single creature, which may refer to a hippopotamus. The Egyptian phrase "ox of the water" sounds a lot like the Hebrew word from which we get "behemoth," but the Egyptians didn't use that phrase. They had another word for "hippopotamus."

Monster: **Cockatrice**

Mentioned in: Isaiah 11:8, Isaiah 14:29, Isaiah 59:5, Jeremiah 8:17

Description: (From Bible) fiery, flying, hatches from eggs. (Traditional) snake-like creature with wings (either eagle-like or leathery), glowing red eyes, and a deadly magical gaze that turns people into stone

Possible Explanations: Most "cockatrice" appearances in the King James Version are rendered either as "serpents" or as specific species of snakes in other translations, but some retain the image of flying. No biblical references to this monster convey the idea of a deadly gaze, just deadly venom. Some translations do add the adjective "fiery." It's more likely that this refers to the burning sensation its bite brings than red eyes that petrify people.

Monster: **Dragons**

Mentioned in: Deuteronomy 32:33, Job 30:29, Psalm 44:19, Psalm 74:13, Psalm 91:13, Psalm 148:7, Isaiah 13:22, Isaiah 34:13, Isaiah 35:7, Isaiah 43:20, Jeremiah 9:11, Jeremiah 10:22, Jeremiah 49:33, Jeremiah 51:34, Micah 1:8, Malachi 1:3, and lots of other places.

Description: can swallow a man, has a head, has a sense of smell, can wail, is okay in water or on land, lives in dens, associated with desolation, is astonishing, hissing.

Possible Explanations: This may be the easiest monster to explain. In a few places not listed above, it's obvious that "dragon" is used as a metaphor— a way to indicate a person who is really horrible (as in Ezekiel 29:3). In other places, dragons are referred to alongside other, indisputably real, animals with no hint of metaphor.

It's likely that such references are poor translations, for in later versions of the Bible, "dragons" in KJV become jackals, hyenas, or snakes. Perhaps "dragon" was a catch-all medieval word for a scary, nasty beast. The KJV is known to have some other translation errors, and all occurrences of "dragon" outside of Revelation disappear in the New KJV.

Isaiah 51:9 does give one dragon a name: Rahab. But we shouldn't read this as naming a literal dragon. Rahab was the name of fictional dragon in Jewish mythology and came to be a poetic synonym for Egypt.

Monster: **Giants**

Mentioned in: Deuteronomy 3:11 and 9:2, Joshua 15:14, 1 Samuel 17, 2 Samuel 21:16, 1 Chronicles 20:4-6

Description: like humans, but larger

Possible Explanations: This monster is the hardest to dismiss. Nine giants are mentioned by name in the Bible: Og, Anak, Sheshanai, Ahiman, Talmai, Goliath, Ishbi-benob, Sippai, and Lahmi. Very specific detail is given for some, including one who had twelve fingers and twelve toes (a rare, but well-documented and still occurring, medical condition known as polydactylism).

Notes:

Notes:

We know for a fact that in modern times Robert Wadlow, from Illinois, was 8 feet 11.1 inches tall and weighed 490 pounds. Zeng Jinlian (a woman) from China was 8 feet 1.75 inches.

And as of this writing, Broc Brown from Michigan is over seven feet tall… at the age of 17!

Unless we limit the term "giant" to creatures as big as houses, then it seems reasonable to accept this biblical "monster" as accurately portrayed.

Monster: **Leviathan**

Mentioned in: Job 3:8, Job 41, Psalm 74:14, Psalm 104:26, Isaiah 27:1

Description: lives in sea; has tongue, head, nose with nostrils, jaw, skin, scales, and teeth; can breathe fire; resistant to weapons; scary-looking

Possible Explanations: This may be the hardest monster to understand. While there is a very detailed description in Job 41, which would indicate an actual creature, there's no verifiably real animal that fits the description. Like "dragon," this may just be a word used to indicate an unknown beast. In fact, Isaiah 27:1 calls Leviathan both a serpent who lives in the sea and a dragon. Maybe it's a now-extinct sea creature.

Maybe it's an embellished description of a whale, orca, crocodile, or shark. The whole breathing fire thing may make us want to consider this monster pure fantasy or extreme exaggeration, but there is in fact a parallel example. The Bombardier Beetle of Central America secretes and mixes two separate chemicals that heat up and combust, sending a tiny explosion out of the beetle's backside to scare off predators. If a beetle can make an explosion, could a large sea animal spit fire?

Monster: **Nephilim**

Mentioned in: Genesis 6:1-4, Numbers 13:33

Description: mighty, large

Possible Explanations: This one has caused lots of speculation. The Bible says the Nephilim were the offspring of divine beings ("sons of God," possibly fallen angels), and human women. Some translations call them giants.

One theory, not very popular, says God sent the flood to kill off these crossbreeds because they weren't part of God's plan for creation. Another, even less popular among scholars, says the Nephilim had something to do with extraterrestrials.

The mention of Nephilim in Numbers may not have actually varified their existence, but was rather just scared spies drawing on old stories in hope of generating enough fear to avoid an armed confrontation.

Monster: **Satyrs**

Mentioned In: Isaiah 13:21, Isaiah 34:14

Description: No description in Bible. Mythological satyrs were part humans and part goat.

Possible Explanations: This monster is almost definitely the result of translation errors. All translations later than KJV use "goats." Some add "shaggy" or "wild." The confusion comes from the Hebrew, which indicates these goats are demonically wild.

Monster: **Unicorn**

Mentioned in: Numbers 23:22, Numbers 24:8, Deuteronomy 33:17, Job 39:9-12, Psalm 22:20-22, Psalm 29:5-7, Psalm 92:10, Isaiah 34:7

Description: (From Bible) untamed, strong, horned. (Traditional) horse-like, one long horn, good, magical, wise, intelligent, virtuous, peaceful, but fierce when needed.

Possible Explanations: Non-biblical Jewish folklore includes unicorns. When Adam and Eve saw their first sunset, they thought creation was being undone. Seeing the following sunrise, they were so joyful they made a sacrifice to God—a unicorn.

This all supposedly happened on the exact spot that became the altar of the Temple in Jerusalem. Medieval Christians used the unicorn as a symbol for Christ.

None of this indicates, however, that any God-follower ever believed in unicorns as we picture them today, only that this creature was accepted as an allegory or metaphor.

Notes:

Notes:

No translation after KJV includes unicorns. The Hebrew word re'em, translated as "unicorn", means "one-horn" and probably refers to a breed of cows, auroch, which went extinct in the 1600s. Other ancient writings mention these animals, but any images are guesswork.

Monster: **Zombies**

Mentioned in: Matthew 27:52-53

Description: animated human corpses

Possible Explanations: We are not going to figure out this one in a few sentences when scholars have debated it for centuries. Maybe the earthquake moved the stones that sealed tombs; when this was later noticed, assumptions were made that the dead had risen.

Maybe it happened exactly as Matthew described it. Maybe Matthew added this event to poetically foreshadow the future resurrection of those who die in Christ. There are many other theories as well. Maybe the truth lies somewhere in between them all.

Theological Underpinnings
There seem to be two groups of people who have far more than a casual curiosity about this subject. One group is comprised of fundamental Christians who believe every word of the Bible is true, inerrant, factual, and scientifically accurate.

They say anything in the Bible not supported by science is due to non-believers corrupting science or science not yet having found the truth. For this group, these monsters highlight the shortcomings of science.

The other group is comprised of non-believers who hate Christianity and want to prove that anyone who believes the Bible is intellectually anemic.

To this end, they, ironically, ignore some simple thought processes, such as realizing that translating ancient texts from one language to another may raise some difficulties, and that some of the things mentioned in the Bible were intended to be allegorical or metaphorical and are generally understood as such.

So we have two groups saying the same thing—"the Bible says all these monsters really existed exactly as described"—but they're doing so for exact opposite reasons.

With this lesson we're not trying to prove the Bible is a science textbook, nor are we calling anybody stupid. Instead, we're having a little bit of fun, scratching our heads, and learning to appreciate that no matter how smart we are (or think we are), we still don't know everything.

Our Confession of Faith says that God is creator of everything, what's known and what's unknown (1.10), so whether a creature existed in the past, exists now, or will exist in the future, we can know that it is God who created it.

Applying the Lesson to Your Own Life

How do you react when you hear or read about a Bigfoot sighting or a Loch Ness Monster sighting? Why do you think you react that way?

Do you need hard evidence to believe something is real? If not, what do you think of those who do? If so, can you think of anything you accept as true without hard evidence?

What are some things that you encounter every day that are a mystery to you? The internet? How your pancreas works? What keeps your heart beating? What are some things that used to be a mystery to you, but you have figured them out?

When you were your students' age, what were some of the big unknown things (in your own life, in the world, in science) that are now common knowledge? Do you think some of today's big unknown things will be common knowledge in the near future?

Notes:

Notes:

Digging Deeper:

There is a writing we Protestants don't recognize as a legitimate book of the Bible, but Roman Catholic Christians do. It's called "Bel and the Dragon," and it's a different version of the Daniel story. In this version Daniel proves the Babylonian god Bel is nothing more than a statue, even though it appears as though Bel eats food offerings left at the feet of his idol every night. Daniel proves that it's the priests and their families, sneaking in through a secret door, who eat the food. The king then says there's no way Daniel can debunk the local dragon as just a statue because, "he liveth, he eateth and drinketh," even though that's pretty much what everybody thought about Bel. And indeed, this writing does not say the dragon wasn't really alive, but that Daniel kills it by feeding it firebombs hidden inside cakes of bread. In this writing, these actions are what lead to Daniel being tossed into the lion's den.

The Lesson

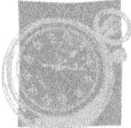

Get Started (10 min.)

Hang up the newsprint, and distribute the drawing supplies.

Explain that you are going to describe an animal, bit by bit, and your students will draw a picture of that animal, based on your description.

Have each student, one by one, come to the newsprint and draw just one of the following characteristics. Each subsequent student will build on others' previous work.

If the size of your class allows it, make sure everyone has a chance to draw. Some may have to take more than one turn in small classes.

Here are the characteristics:
- Has a nose
- Eats grass
- Strong as a lion
- Tail like a cedar tree
- Strong thighs
- Strong belly
- Limbs like iron bars
- Hangs out in the swamp

Have everyone observe the finished picture for a moment, and then say: **So, what kind of animal is this?**

Explain that what you described was from the Bible—an animal called Behemoth.

Say: **Behemoth is just one of the weird, monster-like creatures mentioned in the Bible. Let's take a closer look at it and some others.**

Listen Up (20 min.)

If you don't think you will have enough time to cover all the monsters listed above, choose some to drop. With that introduction, though, you probably should keep Behemoth.

Mix and match from the following options to introduce each monster. You can choose which one, have each student choose, or have a six-sided die for each student to roll, with a 6 meaning "roll again."

Option #1: Repeat the "Get Started" exercise, but have a one student draw the entire monster you describe, and then have the class guess what it is.
Option #2: Name the monster and have a different student draw his or her idea of what that thing would look like, without a description.
Option #3: Privately reveal the name and description of the monster to one student, and have him or her silently do charades in an attempt to get the others to name it.
Option #4: Privately reveal the name and description of the monster to one student and have him or her silently draw a picture in an attempt to get the others to name it.
Option #5: Have each student choose from the above options.

Use the background material above, and for each monster:
- Explain how often it appears in the Bible, and where.
- Share the possible explanations.
- Have students discuss which explanations they agree and disagree with, and offer their own, additional possible explanations.

Now What? (15 min.)

Explain the two extreme positions on this subject, from "Theological Underpinnings," above.

Notes:

Just in Case:
If any of your students really seem interested in the idea of blending monster lore and Christianity, recommend they read the following books: Dwellers by Roger Elwood, Monster by Frank Peretti, The Oath by Frank Peretti, and Many Waters by Madeline L'Engle

Notes:

Ask: **How would you respond to someone who says, "Any creature or monster the Bible mentions had to have existed exactly as it is described"?**

Allow discussion.

Ask: **How would you respond to someone who says, "The Bible says dragons and unicorns are real, but everybody knows they aren't. So, either the Bible lied or it was wrong. Therefore we can't believe anything else in it"?**

Allow discussion.

Ask if anybody knows what a coelacanth (SEEL-uh-kanth) is. If not, explain that this is a kind of fish that was thought to have gone extinct 65 million years ago… until some commercial fishermen caught one off the coast of South Africa in 1938.

Since then, it has been discovered that there are an estimated 1,000 of these fish still alive and well, some off the coast of Africa and some in Indonesian waters. The coelacanth grows to be over six feet long and about two hundred pounds.

Also reveal that according to the International Institute for Species Exploration (part of the State University of New York's College of Environmental Science and Forestry), each year a committee of experts name the "top ten new species discovered" worldwide.

n 2013, nearly 18,000 new species were discovered. The top ten list included mammals, plants, shrimp, lizards, and microbes. Scientists say there are about 2 million species alive right now and estimate there are 10 million more we don't know about yet.

Ask: **When somebody discovers a new species or some species we thought was extinct, does it make you wonder what else we don't know, what else might be out there?**

Allow responses, and elicit discussion especially from any student who responds negatively. Don't try to change anyone's mind here; just try to make them think about this more deeply than immediate reactions.

Ask: **What are some things that you encounter frequently that you fully, or even mostly, understand?** (how a car works, how to do my job, etc.)

Live It (5 min.)

Read aloud the following portion of section 1.10 from the Cumberland Presbyterian Confession of Faith: **"God is the creator of all that is known and unknown."**

Close with this or a similar prayer: **Creator God, we thank you for designing and making everything—those things we know and understand; those things that we don't yet know about and may never know about; and those things that are a mystery to us. We thank you, God, for mystery, for the fun of speculating, and for the curiosity and imagination to try to figure out what we don't know. And we thank you, God, for the faith to accept that which we can't know for sure.**

Resources used: All the Women of the Bible by Herbert Lockyer, cnn.com, deism.com, guinnessworldrecords.com, mythcreatures.co.uk, nationalgeographic.com, Orthodox Jewish Bible, sacred-texts.com, The New Bible Dictionary, thetallestman.com

© 2015 Discipleship Ministry Team of the Ministry Council of the Cumberland Presbyterian Church. All Rights Reserved.

Notes:

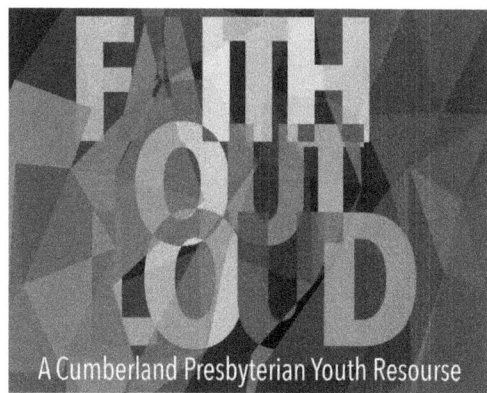

Eat What? Drink What?
by T.J. Malinoski

Scripture: 2 Kings 18:27

Theme: We need to find ways to approach the scriptures that are difficult to understand.

Resource List

- Biblical commentaries such as: The New Interpreters Bible, Word Biblical Commentary, The Westminister Guide To The Books Of The Bible
- News tabloids such as: National Enquirer, People Magazine, and People
- Copies of "Reader's Theater" skit: Eat What? Drink What?

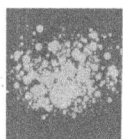

Leader Prep

- Make copies of the skit ahead of time
- Read through different commentaries to familiarize yourself with the passage

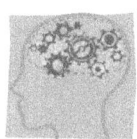

Leader Insight

Connecting to Your Students

By itself, we may find this verse extreme, explicit, vulgar, and offensive. The King James Version of the Bible uses the words "dung" and "piss" when referring to what the people on the wall can do. Most likely, we have not heard a sermon preached, or read a Sunday School lesson, that has made reference to this particular scripture (until now). Two common responses to the verse are to read over it quickly or to ignore it completely. But neither of these responses gives justice to the text and the story behind it. If we allow ourselves to be open to the context, the meaning becomes clearer, even if the abrasiveness of the language remains.

But we may feel like its easier to just look at the verse by itself or to leave it alone completely. By making these conscious decisions, we miss out on a rich and real human aspect that connects us with the scriptures.

Notes:

Explaining the Bible

The scripture for this study comes from the Biblical writers of 2 Kings. This book of the Bible is a continuation of 1 Kings recalling the life of both the Northern and Southern kingdoms: Israel and Judah. A neighboring empire is rising to power and becomes hungry for more land. Assyria moves its army into both kingdoms, conquering and enslaving the people as it moves southward.

Interestingly, the Biblical writers attribute the downfall not to the Assyrian armies but to the people ignoring God's warnings. 2 Kings 17:7 reflects, "This occurred because the people of Israel had sinned against the Lord their God," and in verses 13 and 14, "Yet the Lord warned Israel and Judah by every prophet and every seer saying, 'Turn from your evil ways and keep my commandments and my statutes'...They would not listen but were stubborn, as their ancestors had been, who did not believe in the Lord their God."

By despising God's commandments, the covenant, and God's teachings, the tragedy that has befallen both kingdoms is of their own doing.

Judah, watching the northern kingdom fall into the hands of the Assyrians, attempts to take a different approach. Instead of drawing out a long fought battle, they begin political negotiations, hoping for a peaceful outcome.

King Hezekiah pays a high tribute to the king of Assyria, giving the Assyrians all the silver and gold in their treasuries including stripping down all the valuable metals from Temple. In response, the Assyrian king sends Rabshakeh as a spokesperson, backed by a vast army.

Standing below the city wall of Jerusalem, Rabshakeh challenges King Hezekiah and the people of Judah to complete submission, "Do you think that mere words are strategy and power for war? On whom do you now rely, that you have rebelled against me?" Rabshakeh raises an important question.

Judah no longer has a political ally in Egypt and most likely offended God by stripping the Temple of all valuables to pay tribute to the king of Assyria. Knowing this, Rabshakeh gives King Hezekiah a challenge to emphasize the people's plight. He wagers that even if he gave them two thousand horses, Judah could not stop the army assembled behind him.

Rabshakeh even says that they cannot call on God because from whose Temple did they remove silver and gold from to pay tribute to Assyria. In essence, he says, you can neither turn to Egypt nor your God to save you. In fact, Rabshakeh says, "The Lord said to me, 'Go up against this land and destroy it.'"

All of this sets the stage for the singular text for this lesson. Rabshakeh, spokesperson for Assyria, backed by a mighty army ready for battle, articulates the futility of the people of Judah's situation.

The people of Judah are doomed "to eat their own dung and to drink their own urine." Holding out for peaceful negotiations is futile; fighting back with no real army is futile. Waiting on God whom the people of Judah offended is futile. With no peaceful negotiations or financial payment to give, no army to assemble or protect them, no higher power to intervene on their behalf, the people of Judah are left with nothing but their own human waste.

This is a powerful, demoralizing statement for Rabshakeh to make. In its context, the scripture vividly, if not offensively, makes its point: Give up now and accept your fate or find yourself in a horrible position of doing something that is less than human.

If we were to continuing reading, Rabshakeh promises the people that in surrender, "…then everyone one of you will eat from your own vine and your own fig tree, and drink water from your own cistern, until I come and take you away to a land like your own land, a land of grain and wine, a land of bread and vineyards, a land of olive oil and honey, that you may live and not die."

Do you hear the contrast? Rabshakeh gives the people a stark alternative. Human waste and death, or grain, fruit, wine, water, oil, honey and land. To a people facing possible extermination, or at best, slavery, which sounds more appealing?

With this contextual background, the vulgarity of the text loses some of bite. Its twist of words becomes less untangled. Read chapters 17-19 to get a better idea of the circumstances and outcome of the people of Judah.

Notes:

Notes:

Theological Underpinnings

At face value, Rabshakeh's statement can be construed or interpreted as offensive. When studied more completely with the other chapters of 2 Kings, the reader discovers its meaning and intention more clearly. The words he uses are bold, but they are intended for a particular people, in a particular circumstance, at a particular time. Looking at these "particulars" helps us understand the reason for his words.

The lesson's aim is to help your young people develop methods for discovering the context for what is occurring within the scriptures. The meaning of the text is not always clear when couched in the light of just one verse and we miss the entire meaning(s) when a verse is looked at by itself.

Applying the Lesson to Your Own Life

Part of being a Christian is to grow and mature in the faith. One way in which we grow is through studying the scriptures. When you come across a text that you do not understand, find troubling, or even offensive, what do you do? When faced with this dilemma, we do have resources available to us.

There are numerous Biblical commentaries that can be purchased or found online. Examples include: The New Interpreters Bible, Word Biblical Commentary, or The Westminster Guide To The Books Of The Bible to mention a few. Your church's library may have commentaries available. Many Bibles have study guides and scriptural references to help with historical context and meaning.

Consider consulting your pastor or someone within your congregation that is knowledgeable of the scriptures. Speaking with them may give you insight on a particular text. Your young people are most likely even newer to the faith. They have questions of scriptures like anyone and are perhaps, more open to seek the answer.

Always encourage an openness for asking questions among your group. Do not be afraid to say that you do not know the answer, but treat it as a learning opportunity to make a discovery together.

The Lesson

Get Started (10 min.)

Once the students are seated, pass out various music CDs, DVDs of television and movies, and video game cases of various ratings (example: G-rated, TV-14, R-rated, Mature rating, etc.). Your youth either possess content with, or have seen, these ratings before. After the various media has been passed around, allow the students to comment on the content.

Discussion Questions:

- Who determines the ratings for the music we enjoy, the games we play, and the television and movies that we watch?

Movies: Motion Picture Association of America (MPAA) www.mpaa.org

Music: Recording Industry Association of America (RIAA) www.riaa.com

Video Games: Entertainment Software Rating Board (ESRB) www.esrb.org

Television: Federal Communications Commission (FCC), specifically the TV Parental Guidelines Monitoring Board (TVPGMB) www.fcc.org and www.tvguidelines.org

- How do these associations, boards, and commissions determine the grade/rating that each receive?
- Why is it important to have these ratings?

Notes:

Leader Tip:
If you do not have a wide array of entertainment, ask your youth ahead time to bring what they are currently listening to, watching, or playing. Reserve judgment on content please!

Notes:

Leader Tip:
Have your youth look at other versions of the scriptures to see how they translate 2 Kings 18:27.

Say: **The Bible has lots of scenarios, individuals, activities, and words that could be rated as suggestive dialogue, violence, crude or coarse language, blood and gore, and contain some material that may be inappropriate for children under 13.**

- What do we do when we come across a scripture that fits into one or more of these categories?
- What scriptures can you think of that may fit in one of these categories?

Listen Up (25 min.)

Tell your youth that they will examine a passage of scripture that has some coarse language in it. Hand out copies of the Reader's Theater and choose volunteers to be the readers. The Reader's Theater is inspired by what is happening in 2 Kings 18. If your youth are interested in the conclusion, familiarize yourself with chapter 19, or have them read the chapter before the end of the lesson.

Have students volunteer to play the different parts. Encourage them to go all out and get into it.

After the skit, ask the following discussion questions:

- 2 Kings 18:27 has the verse with the coarse/vulgar language. How did you react when Rebshakeh said those words?
- Should Biblical interpreters or translators stay true the original language of the text, or should they edit the verse and others like it? Why? Why not?
- As Christians, how should we handle verses in the scriptures that contain language, violence, sex, or death that in other situations would probably be deemed inappropriate to discuss?

Leader Tip: Have your youth look at other versions of the scriptures to see how they translate 2 Kings 18:27.

 # Now What? (15 min.)

Remind your youth that taking a sentence or statement out of context is common. We experience it in our personal lives and witness it in various forms of media. Politicians use the words of their opponents against them, news venues use sound bites to relay information, even our texts and use of social media (Facebook, Twitter, Instagram, etc.) can be misunderstood without having a context attached with it.

Misleading, Misguiding, Mistaken, Oh My!

Collect tabloids found in the grocery store like National Enquirer, People Magazine, People, etc. You can also include websites and newspapers to your list.

Pick ones with catchy headlines that are true, misleading, or mistaken. Read, or have your youth read, just the headline and have the group vote if the headline is true, misleading, misguiding, or mistaken.

Also see if your youth can determine the story based solely on the headline. Have fun. Allow humor and creativity during this exercise. Then share with the group the entire story, and emphasize how just a part of the story can be misleading, misguiding, or just plain untrue.

Compare what has been learned from the different forms of media to the lesson's scripture. By itself, 2 Kings 18:27 does not make sense and can be interpreted as extreme, explicit, vulgar, and offensive. Discovering the context Rabshakeh is saying it is important as he uses shock value to his advantage. We know this by studying the text surrounding the verse and its historical context.

Notes:

Notes:

Notes:

Explain that this can happen in our daily lives. Ask, "Have you every sent a text to someone that was misunderstood, misinterpreted, or taken out of context?" (Include in your question Facebook and other forms of social media). What was it like? How did people respond? How did that make you feel?"

Live It (5 min.)

This part of the lesson is two-fold. When studying the scriptures, we have to look for the context in which something is written. Help your youth know that resources like Biblical commentaries, study guides, websites, and one's pastor are available when coming across a scripture that is difficult to understand. Y

ou may want to have some of these available for the lesson. Encourage them to get on their phones (if they have them with them) and find helpful online Bible commentaries.

Encourage your youth to be thoughtful beforehand on the use of social media to avoid misunderstandings and misinterpretations. This can prevent awkward situations and hurt feelings.

Pray: **God your words in scripture inspire and encourage us. Help us when we do not understand their meaning. Help us to seek out direction and insight to help in our faith. Encourage us to be thoughtful in how we communicate with others. Amen.**

© 2015 Discipleship Ministry Team of the Ministry Council of the Cumberland Presbyterian Church. All Rights Reserved.

Reader's Theater based on 2 Kings 18 "Eat What? Drink What?"

Narrator: In a city facing defeat, a vast army surrounds its stone walls. The people of Judah are tired, hungry, and scared. They have given all their silver and gold to their enemy, but their adversary wants more. Rabshakeh, spokesperson for the army and the Assyrian king, approaches the wall of Jerusalem to speak with King Hezekiah to determine the peace treaty.

Rabshakeh: Hezekiah come out! Lay down your arms!

Hezekiah: We have given you all our silver and gold. We've drained our treasuries. We've stripped the gold of the Temple doors. We have done all that was asked of us. Go away! Come again without your army and we can talk.

Rabshakeh: Do you think mere words are strategy and power for war? Who do you rely on now?

Hezekiah: We have an ally in Egypt, you know.

Rabshakeh: Your friends in Egypt will not save you. They are broken like a dry reed on the desert sand. I'll even place a wager with you to make it a fair fight. Come out, and I'll give you two thousand horses. But we both know that you have no one—no one to ride the horses into battle. Admit defeat, Hezekiah, king of Judah, and save your people.

Hezekiah: We are God's chosen people. We have God on our side.

Rabshakeh: You rely on God? Is it not God's Temple from which you removed all that is valuable to pay my king? It is with your same God that I have come up against this place to destroy it. For God said to me, "Go up against this land and these people and destroy them." God is on my side, not yours.

Eliakim, Shebnah and Joah: Please, speak with your army in your native language. Perhaps they will have pity on us and go away.

Rabshakeh: My king has sent me to speak with you, not my army. These words are to all of you who are doomed to eat your own dung and to drink your own urine.

People on the wall: Nooo!

Rabshakeh: People of Jerusalem, do not let Hezekiah deceive you. Make peace with the king of Assyria and come out. Then everyone one of you will eat from your own vine and your own fig tree. You will drink water from your own cistern. I will personally take you to a land like your own where you will have grain and wine, bread and vineyards. A land of olive oil and honey where you may live and not die.

Narrator: But the people were silent, not uttering a word. What happened to the people of Judah? Did their future consist of human waste and death, or lands of prosperity and life? Was Egypt speeding toward Jerusalem on chariots and horseback to save the day? Did God intervene on their behalf? Read on in 2 Kings 19 for the nail-biting conclusion of "Eat What? Drink What?"

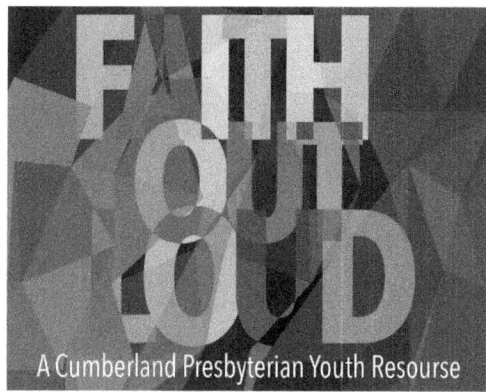

Social Stoning: Are You Without Sin?

by Melissa Reid Goodloe

Scripture: John 8:3-11

Theme: Jesus wants us to realize that only he is without sin, and we all need Jesus!

Resource List

- Markers
- 3 sheets of newsprint
- Tape
- Pens/pencils

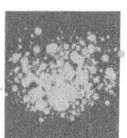

Leader Prep

- Read the scripture; think about what might be considered stone throwing today.

Label newsprint:
  #1 What social media do you use?
  #2 Have you ever embarrassed or made fun of someone on a social site?
  #3 What does it mean to be without sin?

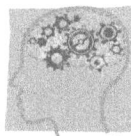

Leader Insight

Connecting to Your Students
With today's social media, a bad picture, tweeting a bit of gossip, or a negative post can seem a lot like a stoning. For a young person, these remarks have the same emotional, hurtful impact as any blow felt physically by a stone. Everything is fine as long as you are on the side flinging stones, but when you are getting hit, it is another story. Today these social stonings do not cause just humiliation and ostracism; some have even ended in death.

Notes:

Explaining the Bible

In this lesson, we explore the outlier gospel. An outlier is defined as "something that lies outside the main body, something that stands apart from others." The Gospel of John is the maverick, non-conformist, unconventional, the outlier Gospel.

Matthew, Mark and Luke are known as the synoptic gospels. There are many similar stories of Jesus found in the pages of all three. Mark is considered to be the earliest Gospel written and it is believed to have been a source for the authors of Matthew and Luke. Are there differences between the three? Yes, but they complement one another so very well that they are grouped together. The Gospel of John however is a totally unique gospel.

There is not a consensus of the authorship of the Gospel of John. Some scholars contend it was John the apostle, some say John the Elder, or some say a variation of the two. Most scholars would date the gospel around 100 A.D., almost 70 years after the death of Jesus and 40 years removed from the Gospel of Mark. This date would also put it 30 years after the fall of Jerusalem and the destruction of the Temple. Another observation is that by the time the Gospel of John was written, Christianity was no longer just a fringe religion, but perhaps it was well established in many areas.

From the very opening words of the Gospel of John, we know this is a very different gospel written for a very different time. We don't begin with a birth narrative or his baptism; we begin at the beginning of all things.

In the beginning was the Word, and the Word was with God, and the Word was God. He was in the beginning with God. All things came into being through him, and without him not one thing came into being. What has come into being in him was life, and the life was the light of all people. The light shines in the darkness, and the darkness did not overcome it. (John 1:1-5)

Scholars contend that this Gospel was written during a time when Gentiles were looking to Christ. They would not have connected so much to the lineages linking Jesus to David or to Judaism. They needed Jesus to connect to their thoughts, customs, and practices. How did Jesus connect to their worldview? From the first verse, John's Gospel seeks to frame Jesus' story in a way that Gentiles would accept.

Looking at today's lesson, it too, is an outlier. Most of the early manuscripts do not include this story. Many of the earliest Christian teachers do not make mention of this story. In the New Revised Standard Version (NRSV) of the Bible this story is put into brackets to separate it from the other text. It was believed to be contested in its inclusion into canonization of the Gospel of John, perhaps because the text may have been perceived to be lenient on adultery. Thankfully, it was included and we can learn from its wisdom today.

A woman caught in adultery was brought before Jesus by the scribes and the Pharisees. According to the Law of Moses found in Leviticus 20:10 and Deuteronomy 20:22, any woman caught in adultery was to be put to death.

Jesus wrote something on the ground twice, but we have no clues from the scripture what he wrote. Jesus said, *"Let anyone among you who is without sin be the first to throw a stone at her."* It was considered a sin to say that you have no sin. This would have been something the scribes and the Pharisees would not do. When Jesus stood back up, they had all left. This scripture shows the mercy that Jesus shows to all. Jesus had no sin. He could have chosen to stone her as the law was written. Instead, he showed her mercy and said, *"Go your way, and from now on do not sin again."*

Theological Underpinnings

Stoning was a common practice among those following the Law of Moses. This would not be the throwing of pebbles or small stones. The stones they threw were heavy, and some would have been considered boulders. There would have been a lot of blood from the rocks hitting their victim. In Acts 7, when Stephen was stoned, the people laid their coats at Saul's feet to keep them from being soiled (from dirt or blood) or torn. Ironically, Paul was stoned and left for dead by the very people he held coats for when Stephen was stoned.

Applying the Lesson to Your Own Life

Have you ever cast the first stone? You may be saying, "I've never thrown a rock at anybody," but stones come in many shapes and forms. A stone today could be a hurtful word, spreading a bit of gossip, or even a malicious Facebook post. So I guess the question is, "Are you without sin?" Matthew 7:3 says, *"Why do you see the speck in your neighbor's eye, but do not notice the log in your own eye?"* Examine your actions this week. Could any of them be described as throwing stones?

Notes:

Notes:

The Lesson

Get Started (10 min.)

Before students arrive, list on newsprint the following questions:

- What social media do you use?
- Have you ever embarrassed or made fun of someone on a social media site?
- What does it mean to be without sin?

As students arrive, have them answer these questions. Once they are done move on to next section.

Listen Up (15 min.)

After students have finished answering the questions, break into small groups. Hand a Bible to each group, and have them read the scripture for this lesson. (John 8:3-11)

After the groups get done reading, have them discuss these questions:

- What kind of things would be considered stoning today?
- Are you without sin?
- Have you ever cast a stone at someone?

Say: **It's easy to point out times when we've been made fun of or embarrassed or when someone has cast the first stone at us. The difficult thing is for us to own up to it when we have done these things to others.**

Have each group share with the entire group their responses from one of the questions or what they wrote on newsprint earlier.

After students share, say: **Now that we have owned our sin we can now ask God to forgive us.**

Say a quick prayer for forgiveness. After you've finished move on to next section.

Now What? (15 min.)

Say: **Change is possible. We don't have to be the ones casting the first stone. We can be more like Jesus. We just have to come up with a plan.**

Talk with students, and think about ways you can end social stoning. Write them on the newsprint you used earlier.

Make a pact as a group to use social media only for positive messages and to stand up for people who are the victims of social stoning.

In their small groups, have them come up with a skit that helps demonstrate what your pact might look like this week. After some time to prepare, ask each group to perform their skit.

Live It (5 min.)

Pray:
**Dear God,
Help us to be better people. Help us to not cast the first stone or any stone. We ask you to be with those who have been victims. Help us to reach others in a positive way.**

Resources used: Bible Gateway

© 2015 Discipleship Ministry Team of the Ministry Council of the Cumberland Presbyterian Church. All Rights Reserved.

Notes:

Leader Tip:
You might want to have a story ready to share of when you have cast the first stone.

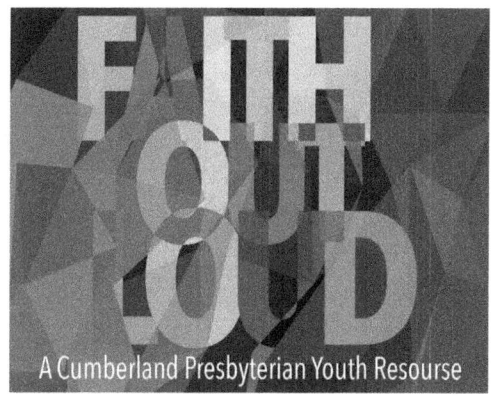

Weird Deaths in the Bible
by Andy McClung

Scripture: Varied

Theme: Death is inevitable... and sometimes weird.

Resource List

- Marker board or newsprint
- Markers
- Pens and pads of paper for students
- Bibles for everybody

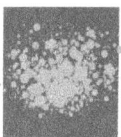

Leader Prep

- Ready a YouTube video for showing

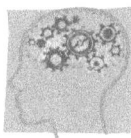

Leader Insight

Connecting to Your Students
North American youth witness death every day through video games, movies, TV shows, and the news. One might think, then, that they are quite familiar with death. But when a peer or loved one dies, many teens are confused and devastated. It's as if they've never even thought about death before.

This dichotomy may be the result of living in a culture that showcases death, via news and entertainment, at an impersonal distance, while striving to separate death from everyday personal experience. Advances in health and medicine prolong life longer and longer. Persons approaching death are put in nursing homes and hospitals, and visited only occasionally: out of sight, out of mind. When death occurs, the funeral home quickly takes the body away; it is only seen again after it has been embalmed and made-up to look lifelike.

Notes:

Perhaps one way to work around this dichotomy, and therefore lessen the devastation felt when this impersonal concept suddenly becomes all too personal, is to make opportunities for youth to think about and talk about death in a safe, non-threatening, low anxiety way. Death experienced as entertainment does not seem to offer such opportunities. While this lesson may approach the entertainment category, it can also offer students this much-needed opportunity to think about death as a real and inevitable part of life.

Explaining the Topic

There is no need to dig deeply into each scripture passage mentioned in this lesson, because the overall focus is only on what these passages have in common: they each feature a weird death.

This lesson can, however, be an occasion for teacher and students to reflect on why we pay attention to some deaths, but not others, in our everyday lives.

Every human being mentioned in the Bible died at some point. (Well, Elijah was carried off to heaven without dying, and there's some debate about Enoch, but those are unique situations.) We don't have reports of the deaths of every single one those people who died, but several deaths in the Bible were unusual or weird enough to stand out.

Thousands of people die every day, but we only hear about a few of them. Why is that? For us to hear about, or pay attention to, someone's death, we either have to know them or know someone directly affected by their death. Maybe we passed the scene of an automobile accident in which someone died, someone died in a store where we shop, etc. Maybe the person who died was famous, or there's something unusual—and therefore newsworthy—about the person or their death.

So, what is it that makes a person's death notable? When the news media report the death of a celebrity, why do so many people feel sad and take to social media to express their mourning?

What makes that death different for people than the hundreds of other similar deaths that happen everyday?

And why do weird deaths draw our attention more than regular deaths anyway? Perhaps for the very reason behind this lesson.

Weird deaths allow us an opportunity to think about and even discuss death, which helps us prepare to deal with deaths later on that will have a personal impact.

In discussing weird deaths of strangers we have a comfortable distance between us and the deceased, as well as the opportunity to focus on the weirdness of the circumstances surrounding the death rather than the uncomfortable concept of death itself.

Theological Underpinnings
Everything dies sooner or later—persons, plants, pets, relationships, businesses, institutions, nations, stars, planets. While this lesson is designed to be fun, it may also prompt your students to think about death as more than an impersonal concept.

One way we learn to deal in a healthy way with stressful and frightening experiences like death is to consider them in a light-hearted, non-stressed way during peaceful times.

It's kind of like why lion cubs stalk and pounce on each other; sure they're having fun, but they're also learning the serious survival skills of stalking and attacking prey.

Similarly, when we humans think and talk about death when our hearts are not hurting over the impending or recent loss of a loved one, we learn to be able to deal better with the trauma when a loved one does die.

Notes:

Notes:

Despite the Old Testament stories used in this lesson, avoid saying that God kills people. This is indeed something we frequently hear at the time of death, though not in those words.

We hear things like, "God needed another angel in heaven," or "God decided to take Momma on home."

Many people are comforted by believing that God micro-manages everything that happens, including deciding who dies, and when, and how. Cumberland Presbyterians do recognize God's sovereignty and omnipotence, but we generally don't believe that God kills people or micro-manages every event in the world.

Applying the Lesson to Your Own Life
How often do you witness death impersonally—on TV, in movies, in books, in the news? Is it so much that you have become jaded?

When you hear of a fatal car accident that tied up traffic for hours, which part of the story hits you hardest, the traffic or the fatality?

How do your reactions vary between the following deaths: a complete stranger, an acquaintance to whom you were not close, someone you knew well in the past but hadn't spoken to in years, someone you didn't know but who a friend of yours knew well, a celebrity you liked, a celebrity you didn't like, and someone you knew well but didn't necessarily love?

Do you react differently to "weird" deaths than you do to "normal" deaths? Why do you think that is?

What would be the weirdest way you can imagine for someone to die (not gruesome, heroic, or spectacular... just weird)?

The Lesson

Get Started (10 min.)

Show the YouTube video entitled "Dumb Ways to Die," posted by DumbWays2Die (3:01). Here's a link: http://www.youtube.com/watch?v=IJNR2EpS0jw. Show this one, the original, rather than one of the trailers for the game, or one of the many spoofs.

Say: **There are plenty of dumb ways to die. There are also some weird ways to die.**

Explain that you are going to share some true stories about people dying in weird ways. The class is to rank them from weirdest to least weird. Choose a student to be the writer. As you read the stories, have this student write on the marker board a simple title for each story (for example: "Molasses," "Fire Hydrant"). After each subsequent story, have the class rank the weirdness of the stories shared so far—weirdest at the top and working down from there.

This may require a lot of erasing and re-writing. Optionally, you could have the student write the titles on large sticky-notes, or index cards with masking tape, and vertically arrange/rearrange them on a wall as the class ranks and re-ranks them.

Here are the weird death stories to share:

Boston, Massachusetts January 15, 1919. A giant vat holding more than two million gallons of molasses ruptured and sent a thirty-foot tall brown tidal wave through the streets, destroying buildings, pushing aside horses and wagons and killing 21 people.

Notes:

Notes:

Oakland, California. June 21, 2007. A new SUV blew a tire, causing it to swerve off the road and hit a fire hydrant. The impact broke the hydrant free and sent it flying through the air. It struck 24-year-old Humberto Hernandez in the head as he walked on the sidewalk with his wife, killing him.

Gloversville, New York, 1994. While playing golf at the Kingsboro Golf Club, 16-year-old Jeremy Brenno made a poor shot on the sixth hole, got angry, and hit a nearby bench with his golf club (a 3 wood). The shaft of the club broke and part of it bounced back and stabbed Jeremy in the heart, killing him.

Norfolk, England, March 24, 1975. While watching a TV comedy show, 50-year-old Alex Mitchell started laughing hard, couldn't stop for 25 minutes, gave one final belly laugh, and died. Turns out, he had a heart condition in which the heart pauses between beats during extreme exertion or excitement. In this case he just laughed a little too hard and too long.

London, England October 17, 1814. A brewery tank ruptured, creating a flood of more than 150,000 gallons of beer that destroyed two houses and killed nine people.

China, August 23, 2014. A chef preparing soup made from cobra meat reached for the head of the cobra—the head that he'd cut off 20 minutes earlier—to throw it away. The severed head bit him. He died before anti-venom could be administered.

Brazil, July 13, 2013. A 45-year-old man was in bed when a cow fell through his roof and landed on him. He died from the injuries. The house backed up to a hill. The cow, unhurt in the incident, belonged to a neighbor.

After the class has ranked these weird deaths, ask: **What's the weirdest death—real, not from a movie or TV show—that you've ever heard about?**

Allow responses. If necessary, guide students away from death stories that are simply shocking or gory and toward those that are truly weird or unusual, such as those just ranked.

Transition to the lesson by saying: **These are all pretty weird. There are some weird deaths in the Bible too.**

 ## Listen Up (15 min.)

Make sure everyone has a Bible. Assign the following scripture passages for students to look up. One by one, have students read aloud these stories of weird deaths. The order does not matter. Allow brief discussion of the stories if students wish, but only to make sure everyone understands what makes the death in the story weird. Make it known that you won't be able to dig very deep into any of the stories.

Genesis 19:24-26. As Lot and his family flee Sodom, which God is destroying, Lot's wife looks back and becomes a pillar of salt.

Numbers 16:28-33. Korah, who had rebelled against God, and those who followed him, are swallowed up by the earth.

Joshua 10:8-11. An army, an enemy of Israel, is killed by hailstones.

Judges 4:15-22, Jael tricks Sisera, an enemy leader on the run, to rest in her tent with a promise to hide him from the Israelite army. Then she nails his head to the ground with a tent peg and mallet.

Judges 9:53-54. Abimelech, embarrassed to be mortally wounded by a woman, orders his armor-bearer to stab him to death before the wound inflicted by the woman kills him.

1 Samuel 4:17-18. Eli dies, upon hearing the Ark of the Covenant has been captured, by falling off of his chair.

Notes:

Notes:

2 Samuel 2:18-23. Asahel is skewered with a spear—the blunt end of the spear.

2 Samuel 11:14-17. Uriah delivers a letter which, unknown to him, contains orders for his own death.

2 Samuel 18:9-15. Absalom, son of David, had fantastic hair. He cut it only once a year. In a battle after usurping the throne, Absalom gets his hair stuck in an oak tree as he's riding by, making him a human piñata.

2 Kings 3:26-27. While losing a battle with Israel, the king of Moab kills his own son as an offering to Moabite gods. This rallies his army enough to drive off the Israelites.

2 Kings 9:30-37. Jezebel, who had led her husband, King Ahab, away from God, is thrown from a window to her death, and most of her body is eaten by stray dogs just as Elijah said it would happen (in 1 Kings 21:23).

2 Chronicles 21:18-19. Jehoram literally spills his guts… well, technically, his guts spill.

Acts 5:1-10. Ananias and Sapphira ignore what all the other Christians are doing (as per Acts 2:43-45), lie about their donation amount to appear generous and righteous, and, when busted for it, drop dead.

Acts 12:21-23. Herod is eaten by worms. Notice the sequence.

Acts 20:7-12. While Paul is preaching a really long sermon, Eutychus falls asleep, falls out a third-floor window, and dies… but he doesn't stay dead.

After all passages have been read, ask: **If we were to rank these weird deaths, which would be the weirdest deaths?**

Allow responses and discussion. Ask respondents to state the reasons for their rankings, but don't actually make a list or force everyone to agree on rankings.

Say: **Do you agree or disagree, sooner or later, everything living thing dies-people, animals, plants, stars, you, me.**

Sooner or later, every non-living thing will come to an end as well—machines, buildings, mountains, relationships, institutions, businesses, nations.

Allow responses and discussion. This is not a forced choice exercise, so don't push students to agree or disagree 100%. Do try to stay out of the discussion as much as possible so students will converse with one another. And don't be afraid of silence.

If it doesn't come up in the discussion at some point, ask about mountains, oceans, and other seemingly permanent physical things. Will even these come to an eventual end? You may also have to clarify that those humans who have entrusted their lives to God through Christ will live again, and for eternity, but they will physically die some day. Angels, though immortal, are not eternal; God created them at some point. God, of course, always has been and always will be.

Now What? (20 min.)

Two options for this portion of the lesson are presented below. If you have a large class, consider dividing students into two groups, having one group follow Option #1 and the other group follow Option #2.

If you have a small group, either choose whichever option you think will work better, or present both options to your class and let students decide.

For either option, take about ten minutes for creating and ten minutes for sharing and/or recording.

Option #1
Have students prepare and present a "nightly news" broadcast which reports some of the weird deaths from the Bible. (Don't worry about the fact that some of them were separated by hundreds of years and many miles.) They can use anchors, in-the-field reporters, eyewitnesses, interviews with coroners or police, or whatever else they wish.

Notes:

Notes:

Try to insure everyone has a part. Consider setting up a mock newsroom. Consider video recording the newscast and posting it on YouTube, GodTube, or your congregation's website or Facebook page. If your class is more into writing than acting, have them create a hashtag and tweets about some of these deaths, instead of creating a broadcast. It may be interesting to see what responses they generate.

Option #2
Have students write and perform a song to the tune of "Dumb Ways to Die," substituting the word "dumb" with "weird" and retelling these stories from the Bible. If you used two or more separate groups, share the song with the whole class. Consider video recording someone, or the whole group, performing the song, and post it on YouTube, GodTube, or your congregation's website or Facebook page. They can either mimic the "Dumb Ways" song exactly ("fall asleep during preaching / just ignore the apostles' teaching") or stray from that format to suit their needs ("Lot's wife decided to halt, and she turned into a pillar of salt.") Rhymer.com or a rhyming dictionary may be helpful. Include your non-singing students by having them prepare and hold up signs with the appropriate scripture passages indicated for each part of the song, or create a cartoon to go along with the song.

Live It (5 min.)

Praise students' creativity and efforts.

Close class with this or a similar prayer: **God, we know death is inevitable, and we pray for all those people who are, right now, sad over the death of a loved one. Help us to better understand and be better prepared for death—the deaths of loved ones and our own deaths.**

Resources used: dailymail.co.uk, snopes.com, telegraph.co.uk

© 2015 Discipleship Ministry Team of the Ministry Council of the Cumberland Presbyterian Church. All Rights Reserved.

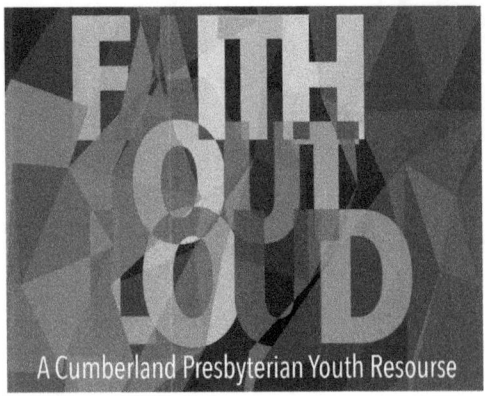

Curses in the Bible
by Andy McClung

Scripture: Varied

Theme: Words matter, and words have power. That's why curses are bad.

Resource List

- Pads and pens for students
- Several Bibles

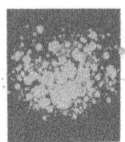

Leader Prep

- If possible, have two adults who are not normally a part of the class attend the first part of the lesson. The less-known to the students these adults are, the better.

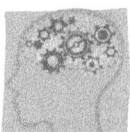

Leader Insight

Connecting to Your Students

Youth live in a world in which many of the words they hear come across much like the teacher's words in those old Peanuts/Charlie Brown cartoons—just a bunch of meaningless sounds. Words today have become not only cheap, but mostly meaningless as well. Social media insure everybody is talking and nobody is listening. Newspersons speak words that have been carefully crafted to send a biased message while appearing to be impartial. Politicians lie to the electorate, get caught, and suffer no repercussions, either claiming that they "misspoke," or they simply shrug off lying as an expected part of politics.

A judge or jury's verdict, based on a close examination of all the available evidence, matters less than what we've already decided about the accused. Teens and children lie to their parents without hesitation. Advertisers make a business out of verbal deception. All of this makes teaching youth the importance of the spoken word in the Judeo-Christian tradition difficult.

Explaining the Lesson
In the Bible, and in Christian theology, a curse is a verbal statement intended to invoke harm upon a particular person or persons. God does some cursing in the Bible, always as a denunciation of sin or a promised consequence of sin. For example, in Deuteronomy 27, God gave instructions about what the Israelites were to do upon entering the Promised Land. The first thing, of course, was to build an altar and offer a sacrifice to God; worship always comes first because it's the most important thing we do. The second thing was to have the Levites—the priests' assistants—remind people of the Law by saying aloud, "Cursed be anyone who…" followed by some point of the law ("makes an idol," "dishonors their parents," etc.), after which all the people were to say "Amen" (which means "so be it") to demonstrate their willingness to follow God's Law. Another more direct example of God actively cursing someone is found in Genesis 3 when, in response to its tricking Adam and Eve into disobedience, God curses the serpent to slither on its belly and always be disliked by humans.

This lesson, however, focuses more on the other kind of cursing—the kind we humans do. And by "cursing" we're not talking about using bad words, although cussing is related to curses, as mentioned below.

There are two kinds of curses made by humans found in the Bible. One is a curse said by one person against another. ("May whoever stole my camel be cursed with hemorrhoids when he rides it.") The other kind is pronounced by a person against themselves should they break their promise or tell a lie. ("May I fall down dead if I break my promise to you." "May I be struck blind if I'm lying about this.")

For ancient peoples, especially the Hebrew people, spoken words were more than just sounds coming out of the mouth; they were agents or ambassadors sent forth, representing the person who spoke them.

Notes:

The more spiritually powerful the speaker was, the more powerful the effect of his/her words. That's why Jesus could heal with a spoken word and kill a fig tree with a spoken curse. It's also why a king's word meant more than a slave's or peasant's. (Kings were believed to be king because the gods willed it.) So, whereas today we might hear an old timer say, "A man is only as good as his word," in ancient times it was also true that a man's word was only as good as the man.

Such a value being placed on spoken words was characteristic of many ancient cultures, not just the Israelites. This was necessary in highly illiterate societies. Don't confuse illiteracy with ignorance or being uneducated, though, for every Hebrew child memorized verbatim the first five books of the Old Testament by the age of ten. It's just that the Israelites, like most cultures, were far more verbal than literary.

In verbal-based societies, things such as verbal contracts, remembering exactly what was said, and telling the truth were incredibly important. Everyone knew this. Almost everyone abided by these beliefs. Everyone knew that without such high respect for the spoken word, their society would be unable to function and therefore would collapse. Those few who chose to lie or break verbal contracts were labelled as untrustworthy and were never believed again. This means they would have had a hard time finding work or engaging in commerce.

To the ancients, spoken words were not only agents or ambassadors of the speaker, but there was no distinction between words and action. If you said something, it was as good as done. This idea was especially prevalent among the Hebrews. Their belief in the power of the spoken word is perhaps most evident in the first chapter of Genesis when God created everything by speaking. That's power! More evidence is found in Deuteronomy 23:23, which says, in part, that whatever one says, one must do.

Theological Underpinnings

Believe it or not, many professional linguists, psychologists, researchers, and authors have studied and written scholarly papers and popular books about foul language (at least in the English language). At least one such recent study has found that in English-speaking societies the average speaker uses cuss words as frequently as pronouns or prepositions. Most people, however, still recognize that it's impolite to use such language in certain situations.

As stated above, this lesson is not about using foul language (swearing, cursing, or cussing), but rather about speaking curses intended to harm someone. These two actions, however, are related. Foul language can be divided into two categories: physical references (bodily functions, sexual actions, etc.), and religious references. Since the purpose of cussing is to be shocking, and bodily functions and sexual actions were not considered private, dirty, or shocking until the 1600s, it's likely that the sacred-effacing cussing developed first. Supporting that theory is that there are no commandments against saying bad words when you stub your toe, but there is one about taking the Lord's name in vain for any reason.

All true cursing is religious in nature because it calls upon a specific deity or unspecified supernatural powers to inflict the intended harm. As for cussing, to say "damn you" or "damn it" originally expressed a desire for someone or something to be truly damned, or sent to Hell, which only a deity can do. This is why cussing is considered bad or rude. Over the years we've shortened this to "damn," often without directing it at a person or object.

True cursing, and its offspring cussing, then, are originally and inherently theological in nature. In ancient times, most people who spoke curses upon someone else did not believe that they, the speaker, had the power to levy a curse. They called upon and relied upon the power of some deity.

Applying the Lesson to Your Own Life
What is the most powerful word you can think of? What makes that word so powerful?

When have you wished you had the power to curse someone or something, like when Jesus cursed the unproductive fig tree? See why humans can only request that deities and other supernatural forces impose curses? If we had the power to do it ourselves, no one would survive. Do you dissuade your students from cussing? If so, is it for social reasons or for theological reasons? What's the difference? Which is more important? Which do you worry about more? What do you think about those Old Testament passages that feature God cursing somebody, or God stating that someone who sins will be cursed?

Take a few minutes and write the absolute worst curse someone could impose on you. Take this with you when you teach the lesson.

Notes:

Notes:

The Lesson

Get Started (10 min.)

Open this lesson by saying: **Finish this sentence: "Sticks and stones may break my bones, but…"**

If none of your students know this old saying, finish it for them ("words/names can never hurt me"). Chances are, even if they do know this saying, your students have not lived by it, as did previous generations. Explain how prominent it used to be, with teachers and parents teaching it to children to help them ignore hurtful name calling by other children. With the increased awareness and sensitivity to bullying now, this sentiment is almost non-existent in school settings.

Ask: **Is it true that words cannot hurt somebody?**

Allow responses, but push for more than simple yes or no answers. Encourage students who believe words can hurt to convince the students who don't—if any—that words can hurt.

Ask: **What are ways that words can hurt?**

You're not looking for anecdotes here, but general situations, such as verbal or emotional abuse, insults and put downs, racist name calling, slander, and just plain meanness.

If appropriate based on the discussion, ask: **What do kids say nowadays to achieve the same effect as the old "sticks and stones" saying? If someone today complained about someone saying mean things, what would other kids say to him or her to convey the same message as "stick and stones"?**

It's likely that at some point during this discussion, a student will say something like, "Words only have the power to hurt us if we allow them to." Affirm such insightfulness, but also challenge the truth behind this statement. Some words, such as racial or ethnic slurs, absolutely carry power in themselves.

Listen Up (20 min.)

Say: **Don't say it aloud, but think of the single, most powerful word you know.**

Choose a few students to share aloud the word they've chosen, even if it's an impolite word to share. If you're worried, you can have students indicate their chosen words without actually saying them. They will know how to do this.

Ask the whole class, after each word is shared: **What makes this word so powerful?**

Ask the whole class if the words they chose are positive or negative. Take a vote, by a show of hands, and announce the totals.

After sharing the totals, whichever side wins, say: **That's interesting, because today we're going to consider powerful words intentionally used negatively. These are called curses.**

If you think it's necessary, briefly explain that the lesson is not about using bad language. If you think it would be interesting to your students, however, briefly share the connection between cussing and cursing.

Have your two unfamiliar adults stand as far apart as possible, facing the students. Tell students that the class will now do a forced choice exercise.

Explain that students who choose the first option should line up, single file, in front of one of these adults, and students who choose the second option should line up, single file, in front of the other. Specify which adult is for which answer. Remind students that they must choose one of the two answers provided.

Ask: **Would you rather... get verbally insulted in public, or get punched?**

After all students have made their choices, ask a few why they chose which answer they did.

Notes:

Notes:

Then say: **Okay, now** (adult) **is going to verbally insult everyone in his/her line and** (other adult) **is going to punch everybody in his/her line.**

Don't go through with this, of course. Instead, thank your adult volunteers and let them leave, if desired. Then ask students who chose the "get punched" line if, had you really gone through with it, they would have wanted to change lines. Ask students who chose the "verbal insult" line if they would have changed.

Say: **If we were in ancient times, it wouldn't matter which line you chose, because both would have been equally painful. In most societies, words and actions were synonymous. Something being said was a good as done, because the spoken word was understood to have a lot of power. This is why the Bible portrays curses so seriously.**

For each of the following passages, have a student read it aloud. Then have the class briefly discuss it. Use the notes below to guide the discussion, but for each passage ask the following questions:

- So, what's the curse here?
- At whom is the curse aimed?
- On a scale of 1 to 10, how bad is this curse?
- How can/could this curse have been avoided?

Genesis 3:13-15. God curses the serpent for tempting Eve to eat the forbidden fruit. Even today, no land animal moves like a snake, and most people find snakes creepy.

Genesis 12:1-3. God will curse those who curse Israel. We protect those whom we love. God loves Israel and will protect it. This promise of a curse doesn't mean God likes cursing anybody, but tries to prevent things from ever reaching that point.

Exodus 21:17 and Leviticus 20:9. Cursing parents is punishable by death. Remember, words were equal to actions. In the ancient world, the survival of your tribe or nation was of utmost importance. If your tribe or nation died, or was captured or overrun, your whole culture disappeared, including your gods. If you weren't killed, you were enslaved and had to assimilate into your conqueror's culture.

Truly cursing your parents (not just saying angry words to them, or cussing at them) threatened the survival of your tribe or nation and was therefore forbidden. Putting to death parent-cursing kids was just cultural self-defense.

Exodus 22:28. Don't revile God or curse your leaders. This passage points to the idea that in ancient times, leaders were assumed to be in positions of leadership (king, queen, general, governor, etc.) because it was God's will. Cursing a God-placed leader was questioning God, or saying that God chose poorly.

Leviticus 20:27. Mediums and wizards shall be stoned to death. Point out that this passage doesn't specifically mention any curse, and ask why it would be included in this lesson. Allow students to arrive at the answer themselves. If necessary, help them along to see that mediums and wizards were the primary persons who claimed to have access to the gods/supernatural powers and could render curses on folks...for a price. This is not God's only problem with mediums and wizards, but this is why this passage is included in this lesson.

Deuteronomy 28:15-46. (Yes, this is a long reading, but should prove to be entertaining.) God details the curse of the consequence of not following God's rules. Again, this is not about God taking joy in cursing anyone, but is about God trying to be proactive here by pointing out the natural and logical consequences of not living the best way possible.

Matthew 25:41-46. The sheep and the goats parable. Jesus says those who do not help those in need are accursed. One of the few cursing references in the New Testament.

Mark 11:12-14, 20-22. Jesus curses, and thereby kills, a fruit-free fig tree. If you used the Faith Out Loud lesson based on this passage (Volume 3, Quarter 2) you may recall that Jesus' action wasn't pointless anger, but based on the fact that only leaves were on the fig tree. It wasn't the right time for figs, but the tree should have had buds. It didn't, meaning that it wasn't going to do what it was created to do—bear fruit. So, the curse and subsequent death happened because the tree wasn't fulfilling its God-given purpose. The tree was "disobeying" God.

Galatians 1:6-9. Paul calls a curse upon anyone teaching a false and contrary gospel. This is similar to the children cursing their parents deal.

Notes:

Notes:

To maintain purity of the one true religion, Paul didn't want those teaching false and contrary religions to confuse or mislead folks trying to follow Christ.

Roman 12:14. Paul says no to cursed others, even our persecutors. This is in keeping with the reduction of curse mentions in the New Testament as compared to the Old Testament. Jesus and his followers were much more interested in love and grace than law and punishment.

Close this portion of the lesson by saying: **It's interesting that there are over 140 occurrences of the word "curse" in the Old Testament, but only 15 in the New Testament. And, most of those in the New Testament are not showing curses as a way God gets things done.**

Ask: **What do you think is the reason for this difference?**

Allow responses without adding much commentary. It's perfectly okay not to arrive at a solid, agreed-upon answer in class. Leaving this question open might inspire some of your students to continue thinking about the lesson throughout the week.

Now What? (15 min.)

Say: **The best curses were the ones that hurt your enemy the worst. So, the more specific a curse was to a particular person or group of people, the better (or worse) the curse.**

Ask: **If someone wanted to customize a curse just for you, what would be the absolute worst curse they could come up with?**

Have each student write the worst curse someone could put on him/her. Not just a bad curse, but the absolute worst. Don't read it aloud, but if you're comfortable doing so, share some details of your own worst possible curse. If you need to use an example to get creativity flowing: "May your PlayStation melt with your GTA4 disc inside, and the fire cause your dog to run into the street and get run over by your girlfriend, whom you never speak to again."

Allow plenty of time for this exercise.

Do not have students read their curses aloud or share their curses with others. One point of this lesson is that words have power, so we don't want to casually toss around verbal curses. The purpose of this exercise is not to be as devious as possible or to put down on paper something someone could use against us, but to force students to consider and identify what is most important to them.

If you have extra time, work as a group to create one or more of the following: a congregation-specific, a community-specific, a state-specific, a nation-specific curse. Again, do not speak the full curse aloud.

Live It (5 min.)

Read aloud the following portion of James 3, from The Message:

A word out of your mouth may seem of no account, but it can accomplish nearly anything—or destroy it! It only takes a spark, remember, to set off a forest fire. A careless or wrongly placed word out of your mouth can do that. By our speech we can ruin the world, turn harmony to chaos, throw mud on a reputation, send the whole world up in smoke and go up in smoke with it, smoke right from the pit of hell. This is scary: You can tame a tiger, but you can't tame a tongue—it's never been done. The tongue runs wild, a wanton killer. With our tongues we bless God our Father; with the same tongues we curse the very men and women he made in his image. Curses and blessings out of the same mouth! My friends, this can't go on.

Then close the lesson with a prayer.

Resources used: prospectmagazine.co.uk, Westminster Dictionary of Theological Terms, The New Bible Dictionary

© 2015 Discipleship Ministry Team of the Ministry Council of the Cumberland Presbyterian Church. All Rights Reserved.

Notes:

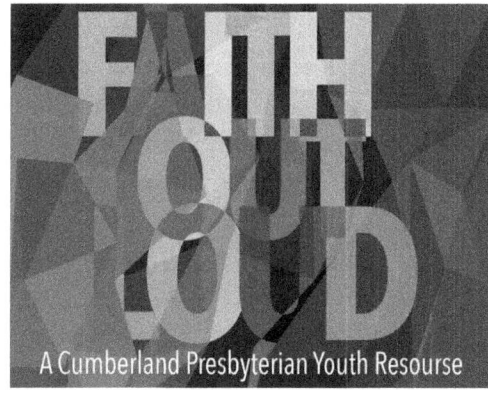

Weird Sexual References in the Bible
by Andy McClung

Scripture: Varied

Theme: The Bible mentions sex a lot, and some of it is just plain weird.

Resource List

- Bibles
- A lockbox or other container that can be securely closed
- Marker board / newsprint and marker

Leader Prep

- Preview the suggested videos, prepare one for showing
- Read the featured scriptures
- (Optional) collect stupid warning labels, or images thereof
- You may want to let parents know the subject for this lesson just to be transparent with them. If they wish, you may need to outline the lesson for them.

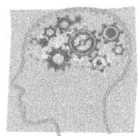

Leader Insight

Connecting to Your Students
Teens are great at spotting a sexual double entendre, and instilling sexual references into completely non-sexual words and phrases. The art of creating dirty phrases out of innocent ones became very mainstream when The Office re-instated the double entendre producing "that's what she said" into society after originally being used in the Wayne's World movie. If you've ever wondered why teens giggled at a certain phrase, and wouldn't tell you why, the phrase probably had a sexual meaning in current teen slang. Spend a few minutes on urbandictionary.com and you'll be surprised. (Be aware, though, many entries there are situation specific or intentionally false, meant as jokes.)

Notes:

Leader Tip:
For a more serious lesson on sex, use "Sex: One of God's Best Ideas" from Faith Out Loud, Volume 1 Quarter 2.

Teen slang changes quickly and often as adults begin to catch on. Additionally, teen slang is sometimes intentionally ambiguous to keep adults confused. Think back to your teen years and you'll surely remember some sexually-charged phrases that your parents and teachers didn't have a clue about.

Some of the sexual references in the Bible, however, are so obscure or just plain weird, that even teens may not recognize them. Other sexual references have been ignored or misused, all in order to claim Biblical support for particular ideas about sex. This lesson is not intended to be awkward or uncomfortable, but fun and affirming to your students that the Bible speaks about relevant things.

Explaining the Bible

You can't read far in the Old Testament without noticing that even the heroes of Judaism engaged in sexual activity that would probably keep them from running for public office today (or, at least, give their opposition plenty to work with.) You can't read far in the New Testament without meeting a virgin or a prostitute, or finding a mention of adultery. Some references to sex are necessary to tell the story. Other references detail rules about sex—rules from both God and humans. So the Bible mentions sex a lot. Most everybody knows this, even if some won't admit it.

The Israelites talked about sex so much because they were a small nation. Back then all it took was a few battles or one epidemic disease and an entire people would be wiped out. Besides that, a broken bone, harsh weather, or a simple infection could lead to death. Making lots of babies was the only assurance that your lineage and your nation continued. Also, they believed they were supposed to keep reproducing because they were God's chosen people; the more Hebrew people, the more people who would praise God. Besides, without all that reproducing, the Messiah would never have been born.

The Bible actually talks about sex a lot more—yes, more—than it appears at first. And many of those references to sex are rather unusual.

Don't be afraid to speak openly and honestly about sex with your students. It may be easier for them to talk with you than their parents. Plus, Christian leaders avoiding talking about sex just conveys to youth that sex is bad or dirty, which is the exact opposite of what God intended.

And it's not like your students don't know about sex. Some of your students probably know about Oholah and Oholibah in Ezekiel 23:1-20 (they won't remember the names, but they'll remember verse 20). They know what Solomon used those concubines for. They've scoffed when told that Jacob didn't know which sister he was having sex with on his first wedding night (Genesis 29:15-25). They may also have discovered The Song of Songs/Song of Solomon, which makes almost 40 metaphorical references to genitals, both male and female, and many poetic references to various sex acts. It is a common subject at school, and, thanks to late night cable TV and the internet, your students are much more aware of weird or unusual sexual practices than you probably were at their age.

Nevertheless, some of the Bible passages covered in this lesson may have slipped under their radar. If any of these passages have ever been used in a worship service, Sunday school lesson, or youth group meeting your students participated in, the sexual element was probably ignored.

Genesis 1:28. After blessing the newly-created first humans, the first thing God says to them is, "Be fruitful and multiply." Until recently, there was only one way humans multiplied: sex. So there it is, the Bible mentions sex on the very first page. Sex is an integral part of being human. It's not a taboo subject in the Bible and shouldn't be taboo in churches or Christian homes. In fact, having sex to make babies is a command from God. Other passages do, of course, add some parameters.

Genesis 24:2-4 and 47:29 both show a Jewish man (Abraham and Jacob, respectively) asking someone to put their hand under his "thigh" to make a solemn promise, like we ask people to place their hand on the Bible in courtrooms today. "Thigh" is a nice way to refer to private parts—the private parts of a Jewish man.

Notes:

Notes:

With no Bible to swear on, it was customary to swear on the thing that indicated a covenant with God: a circumcised penis. This act was called The Oath of the Circumcised Penis. There was absolutely nothing sexual about this practice, but it's weird enough for us to fit this lesson.

In Genesis 26:6-11, Isaac and his wife Rebekah are living in a foreign land. Isaac says Rebekah is his sister so no one will kill him to take her. When the king sees them making out, he's grossed out until he realizes the truth. Isaac learned this trick from his dad, Abraham, who did it twice. The second time (Genesis 20:1-3), the king was preparing to marry and have sex with this supposedly single woman when God intervened. The first time, however (Genesis 12:10-19), it's never stated that the king kept his pants on.

Many presumably well-meaning adults have used the story of Onan, in Genesis 38:8-10, to warn teens against masturbation, but this story never even mentions masturbation. It's a classic case of someone forcing scripture to say what they want it to say. Judah's son Er dies married, but without kids, so Judah tells his second son, Onan, to impregnate Er's widow, Tamar. If a brother died and left his wife childless, it was the duty and responsibility of the other brother to take his sister-in-law as a wife and give his late brother sons so that his lineage would continue. It also protected the vulnerable widow (Deuteronomy 25:5-6). Onan apparently didn't mind having sex with Tamar ("go in to her" is used frequently to mean sexual intercourse), but he didn't want to impregnate her, so he always ejaculated on the ground instead of inside her. He knew any kids born to Tamar would be considered Er's, not his, and they'd probably get Er's portion of the inheritance. With no Er offspring, Onan would get more.

Exodus 20:14, 17. Sex was on the first page of the Bible, and now sex makes it into the best-known portion of the Bible—the Ten Commandments. Twice! Adultery by either husband or wife, either before or after marriage, can confuse and muddle a family's lineage, which was super-important for economic and social reasons. Coveting your neighbor's wife or servant can be for something other than sex, but it does include sex. And, according to Jesus in Matthew 5:28, Jesus knew that repeatedly imagining something—lusting—makes it a lot easier to do that thing, which is why athletes today "visualize" making the shot or crossing the finish line.

Exodus 22:19, Leviticus 18:23, Leviticus 20:15-16, and Deuteronomy 27:21. Warnings against bestiality. You've got to wonder why any set of laws would need to have this included, and repeated three other times! Some people are just gross, of course, but was zoophilia so rampant in ancient Israel that a prohibition against it had to be repeated? Probably not. But the ancient Hebrews were surrounded by many other cultures in which such things happened sometimes as worship rituals to false gods. God and the Hebrew leaders just wanted to make sure that God's people knew that something being popular does not make it right in God's eyes.

Leviticus 21:7 says priests shouldn't marry prostitutes. Maybe this was a trend at some point, but more likely it was a way to keep the Jewish priesthood distinguished from other ancient religions in which priests not only married prostitutes, but priests and priestesses served as "sacred" prostitutes in their gods' temples with sex as part of their worship services. Also, all Jewish priests were in the line of Aaron (Moses' brother). Any child born to a prostitute after marrying a priest could not be guaranteed to truly be in Aaron's line.

Deuteronomy 25:5-10 details a weird Hebrew law: a man is obligated to marry and impregnate his childless, widowed sister-in-law. It's called "levirate marriage"; we see it in the case of Onan above, in Ruth's story, and behind a tricky question to Jesus in Luke 20:27-33. Keeping one's family and lineage going to obey God's first command to humankind, as well as strengthening the tribe and nation, was of utmost importance to the Hebrew people. Levirate marriage also assured that a widow would be taken care of financially.

One bizarre-sounding rule is found in Deuteronomy 25:11-12. Protection of a man's genitalia in a fight. This one has never been used as a Sunday school memory verse! It's obviously part of a male-dominated/female subservient society, but it serves an important purpose. This punishment in this rule seems uncharacteristically disproportionate to the offense. Maybe it was to protect a man's ability to procreate; a serious enough "seizing" could do irreparable harm. Maybe it was to keep women subservient; let one woman do this without punishment and you might have gangs of genital-grabbing women bullying all the men. Maybe it was about the shamefulness of a woman intentionally touching another man's genitals—not sexual, but just too close to adultery. Maybe it was some combination of these reasons.

Notes:

Notes:

For the punishment, though, "hand" (like "feet" or "thigh" or "belly") is sometimes used to refer to genitals, and the Hebrew word for "cut off" can also mean "to shave." So, maybe a woman's punishment for crotch-grabbing was a bikini-wax, which was considered a public humiliation. The punishment fits the offense better.

Ruth 1:16 is used in many weddings even though Ruth originally said it to her mother-in-law, but that's not the weirdest thing in this story. Ruth, a Moabite, married a Hebrew but was widowed before having children. She moved back to Jewish territory and, under the advice of her Hebrew mother-in-law, threw herself at Boaz. The weird stuff happens in Chapter 3. When you read it, it sounds sweet and fairly innocent, but Ruth may have been hoping Boaz would impregnate her. In ancient Judaism a woman's main goal in life was to have a bunch of babies to carry on her husband's bloodline. A widow, Ruth could still honor her husband by getting pregnant from his closest kin. Boaz, however, was a gentleman about the come on. In the end they did get married and have kids.

In 1 Kings 12:3-14 we see King Rehoboam move from inheriting a united Israel to being king only of the southern portion, Judah. What happened? Rehoboam asks the old men how he should lead, and then asks the young men how he should lead. The old guys say he should be a servant to the people and they will, in return, serve him. The young guys say to force the people to serve him, and they suggest a speech that includes the phrase, "My little finger is thicker than my father's loins," his father being the previous king, about whom the people have complained. "Finger" here is probably a nice way to translate "penis." So, the young guys encouraged Rehoboam to belittle his father, exaggerate his own virility, and basically be a big jerk. He took their advice and the kingdom split.

Song of Songs, or Song of Solomon, is basically one long, erotic love poem, possibly written by Solomon, possibly written about Solomon. People have tried to tone it down by saying it's an allegory for the relationship between God and Israel, or Christ and the Church, but that's probably just embarrassment. Teens may get a kick out of the similes meant as compliments in 4:1-5 and 5:10-16.

Theological Underpinnings

On the first page of the Bible, God tells humankind to multiply, which occurs through sex. Sex is good; God invented it. But, as sinful human beings, we misuse this gift. Part of that misuse is not following the rules about how to properly use this gift. Another part is coming up with new ways to misuse it, ways which there are no rules against, but which nevertheless go against God's wishes. The Bible does not hold rules about every conceivable sexual sin. How could it? It seems like we humans are capable of an infinite number of ways to misuse sex. Even the heroes of the faith misuse sex. Our moral and spiritual failures don't change what are right and wrong ways to use sex, nor do they change that sex is good, a gift of God. All they do is distance us from God and hurt both ourselves and others.

Plenty of people have said that humans are closest to being like God when we create a new life through sex. (Actually, we're not creating anything new, we're just putting together what God created, but it's still a good point.) Plenty of people have come to understand God's unconditional love fully (or as fully as we can) only after becoming parents.

Sex is an important part of life. Since the Bible deals with real life, it stands to reason that sex would be mentioned a lot in the Bible. What's surprising, though, is how many of those passages are weird.

Applying the Lesson to Your Own Life

Are you comfortable or uncomfortable talking about sex in church? Why? If uncomfortable, does focusing on what the Bible says about sex make it any easier? Why?
Recall some of the sex-related slang terms you and your peers used when you were your students' age. Did adults know what these terms meant? Are any of those terms still in use? Why do you think some slang endures and some falls into disuse?

What are some sexual practices that were once, within your lifetime, considered weird or unacceptable, but have since lost that stigma for many people? Do you think this greater acceptance pleases God? What happened to change people's attitudes? What are some sexual practices that you think will always be considered weird or unacceptable?

Notes:

Notes:

Do your pastor, your session, your congregation, and/or the people of your community seem to consider sexual sins as somehow worse than other sins? Do you? Why do you think some people do this? Why do you think some people don't?

The Lesson

 ## Get Started (10 min.)

Show one or more of the following YouTube videos.

- "Strange warning labels" (4:19), posted by Harvest: Greg Laurie. Here's the link: https://www.youtube.com/watch?v=Wvo11ClJN4Y
- "Donny & Marie…Warning Labels" (4:21), posted by galofOs. Here's the link: https://www.youtube.com/watch?v=MgOsZx5WbCg (you can start this one at 1:10)
- "World's Dumbest Warning Labels" (9:05), posted by StosselOnFBN. Here's the link: https://www.youtube.com/watch?v=7XzCf3Ayz9w (you can start at :38 with this one and stop at 5:38)
- "Wacky Warning Label 2012 Winners Announced! With Bob Dorigo Jones" (6:58), posted by Politichicks (you can stop this one at 5:15)
- "Funny Warning Labels" (1:26), posted by April-isamommy. Here's the link: https://www.youtube.com/watch?v=zhLy3NZw46U.

If you do not have the ability to show YouTube videos, you could be on the lookout in the week before class for similar stupid warning labels and take photos of them to share in class.

After showing the video(s) or sharing your photos, ask: **What similar warning labels or signs have you seen?** (These should be things that any normal, rational person should not need to be warned about.) Why do you think manufacturers put warnings about such obvious dangers on their products?

Provides this answer if no one else does: **Whether it's the result of previous lawsuits or the fear of possible lawsuits, it all started with people doing things that caused harm to themselves or others.**

Transition to the lesson by saying: **A lot of what the Bible says about sex started the same way.**

Before moving on, though, say that you want to make sure everyone is comfortable talking about sex, so you're going to pass around a lockbox. Each student is to symbolically place his or her embarrassment into the box and leave it there for the whole class time. This way, no one will miss out on learning something because they were too embarrassed to ask questions or make comments. Anyone who wishes to may retrieve their embarrassment on the way out.

Once everyone has held the box for a moment, close it securely and set it aside. But leave it in view as a reminder that everyone's embarrassment is locked away. Make sure that no one is ridiculed for being embarrassed when talking about sex.

Listen Up (20 min.)

There are probably more passages detailed in the "Explaining the Bible" section, above, than you'll be able to cover in class. Let your students' interest guide how much time you spend on each passage.

Explain that the lesson today covers weird things the Bible says about sex.

For each scripture passage listed below, or each that you use in class:

- Have someone read it aloud
- Ask: **What do you think this passage is talking about?**
- Reveal the sexual references, as detailed in the corresponding portion of "Explaining the Bible."
- Ask: **Does this change how you hear this passage? If so, how? If not, why not?**

Notes:

Notes:

- If the passage references a Judaic rule about sex, ask: **Do you think this is one of those rules, or warning labels, that was made because someone did it, or was it God telling people how best to use the gift of sex? Was it proactive or reactive?**
- Also ask any additional discussion questions listed below for each passage.

Genesis 1:28. **If sex is mentioned on the first page of the Bible—as a commandment from God—why do we talk about it so little in church, or why do we only hear negative things about it in church?**

Genesis 24:2-4 and 47:29. **Aren't you glad we don't do that anymore? How can one person touching another's privates not be sexual?**

Genesis 26:6-11, Genesis 20:1-3, Genesis 12:10-19. **Do the women seem to have a say in any of these decisions? Do these husbands seem heroic or cowardly? Do you think Pharaoh and Sarai had sex?**

Genesis 38:8-10. **Who has ever heard this passage used as a warning about masturbation? Why do you think Onan died?**

Exodus 20:14, 17. Matthew 5:28. **Do you have to be married to commit adultery?** (No, because adultery is sex with anybody besides your spouse. So if you're not yet married it's cheating on your future spouse.) **Have you ever heard a coach or somebody talk about "visualizing"? If so, how does that relate to what Jesus said? Besides sex, why might someone covet their neighbors spouse or servant?**

Exodus 22:19, Leviticus 18:23, Leviticus 20:15-16, and Deuteronomy 27:21. **Why do you think this rule is repeated four times in scripture?**

Leviticus 21:7 **How does this rule fit with the whole idea of forgiveness and being cleansed of sin? Would it be forbidden for a pastor today to marry a prostitute? If so, would the reasons be the same?**

Deuteronomy 25:5-10. **Which seems more important in this law, continuing a man's lineage, or making sure a widow is cared for?**

Deuteronomy 25:11-12. **Choosing from those "maybes," or giving an original answer, why do you think they had this law? Do you think the original punishment was cutting off a hand, or shaving the privates? Why? If you can, as some anthropologists say, know something about a society by studying its laws, what does this law tell you about ancient Judaism?**

Ruth 3. **Scripture isn't clear. Do you think Boaz and Ruth had sex on that threshing floor? Why?**

1 Kings 12:3-14. **Why do you think Rehoboam, a young man, took the young men's advice instead of the old men's? Was this a wise decision? Why are guys so obsessed with the size of their genitals? This scene happened about 3,000 years ago. Do guys still try to insult each other by saying "mine is bigger than yours"? If so, why?**

Song of Songs / Song of Solomon 4:1-5 and 5:10-16. **Would describing a guy or girl like this today be romantic and sexy? If not, what metaphors would be? What do you think of this book? Why do you think it made it into the Bible, even though it never mentions God?**

Now What? (15 min.)

Break out the marker board, and select someone to write on it.

Ask: **What are some euphemisms for sex organs or sex acts that we heard in those scriptures?**

Have a student write them on the board as responses are given. Allow students to look up passages again if needed.

Notes:

Just In Case:

If a student asks about ancient Jewish men having multiple wives, assure him or her that while it was a common practice in ancient times, and something engaged in by some God-following Hebrew men, the Bible never says it's okay. In fact, in Deuteronomy 17:14-20, when God is listing the things the Hebrew kings shouldn't do, "acquiring many wives" makes the list. People, even good people, sometimes do things against God's wishes. Not everything the heroes of the Bible do is good or right.

Ask: **Are there others in the Bible you can think of?**

Have a student write any responses on the board.

If you have several words on the board, that's good enough. Potentially, you could have all of the following for genitals: secrets, stones, loins, thigh, privy member, the place of the breaking forth of children, feet, hands, our uncomely parts, and belly. (And "seed" for semen.) For sexual intercourse, you could have: go in unto, go in to, to know someone, to uncover his/her feet, to uncover his/her nakedness, and lie with. There may be variations in both categories, depending on the translations used.

Have students vote for the weirdest euphemism, the funniest, and the one closest to today's slang. Have someone circle these on the board.

Point to all these euphemisms and then ask: **Why can't the Bible just name reproductive organs, or say "These two people had sex"?**

If you've really locked away your embarrassment for this time period, and if you're brave enough, you could carry this discussion a bit further by noting how silly some of these euphemisms sound, and saying that current euphemisms are just as silly-sounding.

Then have students write currently-used sexual euphemisms on the board so everyone can see how silly they are. From these, you could also vote on the weirdest and funniest.

If time allows, you could hold a debate over which of the "winning" euphemisms from each time period (Biblical and current) are the weirdest and funniest.

You'll probably want to erase the board immediately after class.

Live It (5 min.)

Close the lesson by saying: **Real life involves sex, and sometimes that sex is a little weird and not done according to God's wishes. The Bible is about real life, so there is some weird sexual stuff in it. Thank God, the Bible is connected with real life.**

Prayer: **Thank you, God, for the Bible, even the weird stuff in it. Thank you for the Bible being true and honest, and dealing with real life stuff, even when it's weird, or ugly, or scary, or uncomfortable. Help all people better understand and live by your special plans for sex. Amen.**

Resources used: Deuteronomy by Patrick Miller, First and Second Kings by Richard Nelson, The Uncensored Bible by John Kaltner, Steven McKenzie, and Joel Kilpatrick

© 2015 Discipleship Ministry Team of the Ministry Council of the Cumberland Presbyterian Church. All Rights Reserved.

Notes:

That's Not in the Bible?!?
by Andy McClung

Scripture: Vaired

Theme: Some things we think are found in the Bible aren't actually there.

Resource List

- Bibles
- Copies of the handout "That's Not In the Bible"? one per student
- Pens, one per student
- Copies of "Is This in the Bible"? Pop Quiz, two per student
- Envelopes, one per student
- Pads of paper, one for every 2-3 students
- Enough space for break-out groups to work

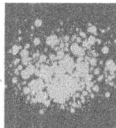

Leader Prep

- Put one copy of the "Is This in the Bible"? Pop Quiz in each envelope and seal them.

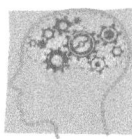

Leader Insight

Connecting to Your Students

Teens seem to enjoy being critical of everything—"critical" here meaning "inclined to find fault with something, often too readily." Nowadays, though, many teens don't seem to have much inclination, capability, or opportunity to be critical of anything—"critical" here meaning "skillful judgment/assessment as to something's truth, merit, or value."

For example, let's say a new movie opens tonight. That movie was likely announced more than a year ago. Teaser trailers and full previews have been shown constantly for the last eight months. Plot details, set photographs, and allegedly pirated video clips have been posted and reposted online thousands of times, and viewed millions of times. Bloggers and fans have already given the movie their thumbs up or down, before even seeing it.

Notes:

A couple of months ago, the studio gave a special early screening to professional critics, and they've published their reviews. So when teens sit down in that movie theater tonight, they've already been primed to like or dislike the movie.

Essentially, they've been cheated of the opportunity to experience and critique the movie for themselves. Constantly being cheated of this opportunity, they've never even learned how to critique movies.

This lesson, hopefully, provides an opportunity for teens to be critical (the finding fault kind) of certain misconceptions about what's in the Bible, while also encouraging them to be critical (the skillful assessment kind) of what's behind those misconceptions.

Explaining the Bible
Presented here is the same information from the "That's Not In the Bible?" handout, with additional notes to help you lead the discussion during the "Listen Up" portion of this lesson. This section, then, is longer than usual. Don't worry; you don't have to cover all of this information.

This lesson will cover three categories of things people mistakenly think are in the Bible: 1) physical things and/or their descriptions, 2) events and their details, and 3) sayings.

- Physical Things
Many people think that particular Bible-related physical items actually existed and therefore must be mentioned in the Bible, when they really aren't mentioned anywhere in scripture. Some of these physical things or beings are indeed mentioned in the Bible, but the generally held descriptions of them are not. These misconceptions and false images come more from art and poetry than from scripture.

The serpent in the Garden of Eden wasn't Satan. Genesis never states this. The idea of Satan as a tempter wouldn't even come along until 500 years after Genesis was composed. This idea probably came from our knowing Satan is evil, and our wanting to blame our sins on a tempter instead of acknowledging our weakness. (Genesis 3:1-15)

The forbidden fruit of Eden wasn't an apple. It could have been, but Genesis never states this; it's only called "fruit." This idea probably came from paintings of the scene as artists imagined it. A bright, red apple draws attention. (Genesis 3:1-6)

Angels aren't female, don't have wings and halos, and don't play the harp. The study of angels is too complicated to fully cover here, but all the mentions of angels in scripture refer to beings who look like men. They're bright, but don't have halos. The angels mentioned in the gospels are not said to have wings. The seraphim have six wings. See Isaiah 6. The typical image of an angel comes from painters. John Milton's Paradise Lost gave us the idea of angels playing the harp. Cherubs, the fat baby angels, are anything but cute. This image probably started when Renaissance sculptors adorned children's graves with images of dancing babies. Ezekiel describes cherubs (or cherubim) in Ezekiel 10:20-22. They have wings.

We don't each have a guardian angel. The Bible shows them bringing messages from God (Luke 1:26-38), fighting fallen angels (Daniel 10:10-14), and helping people (Daniel 6:22). The idea of personal guardian angels probably comes from Matthew 18:10.

People do not become angels after dying. There is nothing like this anywhere in scripture or in 6,000 years of Judeo-Christian teaching. Angels are immortal spiritual beings created by God separately from humankind. This idea was presented in a 1946 children's book, The Littlest Angel and in the 1946 movie "It's A Wonderful Life," but it probably predates both of those. The idea possibly comes from confusion about departed loved ones "watching over us" from heaven; the human inability to let go of departed loved ones; or a comforting idea of what happens to people when we die.

Satan isn't red, doesn't have horns, doesn't carry a pitchfork, and doesn't live in hell. There is no physical description in the Bible, but something that looked like this would have a hard time tempting most people to anything! All these ideas accumulated from images made by various medieval artists trying to visually depict evil. In Matthew 25:41, a character in a parable says hell was prepared for the devil, but not that he lives there.

The Holy Grail doesn't exist. Sure, Jesus used a cup at the last supper (Matthew 26:27) —the Passover meal uses five cups—but there wasn't anything extraordinary about it. The Grail and its magic powers were simply plot devices for the originally French story of King Arthur. The tale has been added to and changed countless times.

Notes:

Notes:

- Events

Many people mistakenly think specific details of certain events are mentioned in the Bible. This may be because so many artistic depictions include those details.

Scripture tells us a large fish swallowed Jonah. It doesn't say a whale, though it may have been one. Whales, of course, are mammals rather than fish, but those who first repeated and eventually wrote down Jonah's story may not have bothered to make that distinction. A whale may be mistakenly attributed to the story simply for its size. (Jonah 1:17)

Baby Jesus being born in a stable may or may not be accurate. The Bible only says he was put into a manger, which leads us to the (admittedly safe) assumption that the birth happened in a stable (Luke 2:6-12). Stables in that place and time were likely to be caves with a gate rather than freestanding structures. Also, the innkeeper who turned away Mary and Joseph is not mentioned in scripture, despite being portrayed thousands of times in Christmas pageants, sometimes as a greedy man who turns them away because they have no money, and sometimes as a compassionate man who allows them use of his stable. Either way, it's supposition.

There might have been more than three wise men, there might have been fewer; the Bible never gives a number. The idea of three probably comes from the three gifts they brought, but has been reinforced by tradition and a hymn, even to the point of giving them names, ascribing them ethnicities, and deciding who gave which gift. (Matthew 2:1-12)

Jesus didn't wear underwear on the cross. The Roman practice was to strip the victim naked, adding to his humiliation. Besides, scripture clearly says the soldiers divided up his clothes. The loincloth, not a Jewish undergarment, was probably added by artists for modesty's sake. (Matthew 26:35, Mark 16:24)

Saul/Paul may or may not have been on a horse when he was struck blind. Artists like to show him dramatically having just fallen off a horse, but scripture only says he fell to the ground. (Acts 9:1-9)

- Sayings

Many people mistakenly think certain Bible-sounding and churchy-sounding sayings are in the Bible. This may be because churchy, Bible-quoting people often use and repeat such sayings.

It may also be that we like bite-sized, easily-remembered, profound sayings. Some of these misquotes are simply paraphrases of real scripture. Some of these paraphrases are used to mean approximately the same thing as they do in the Bible, and some are not.

"A fool and his money are soon parted." Usually true, but not in the Bible. The phrase entered English after 1557, as a condensed form of a rhyming couplet from a poem called "Five Hundred Points of Good Husbandry," by Thomas Tusser, which read, "A foole and his monie be soone at debate / which after with sorrow repents him too late."

"Ask Jesus into your heart." This phrase, popular in some areas, isn't wrong, but it doesn't accurately reflect scripture or Cumberland Presbyterian theology. It probably comes from Revelation 3:20, and the subsequent paintings and hymns. Read it and you'll see that it's a big jump from that verse to salvation. Salvation does indeed come through Jesus. John 3:16, Acts 16:31, and plenty of other passages testify to that, but the key word is "believe." Salvation comes from God's grace. Our part is repentance, belief in Christ as Savior, and following Christ as Lord or master. Our Confession of Faith affirms this in 3.10. "Asking Jesus into your heart" is an oversimplified way of saying all this.

"Cleanliness is next to Godliness." Not in the Bible. It's possibly paraphrased from the Talmud (an ancient collection of Rabbinic teachings), and/or a sermon by John Wesley (1703-1791). Many passages in the Old Testament do emphasize physical, ritual cleanliness before approaching God. New Testament emphasizes spiritual cleanliness. See 2 Corinthians 7:1. This saying is sometimes misused to keep those responsible for cleaning house humbled or subservient.

"God helps those who help themselves." Not in the Bible. Attributed to Poor Richard's Almanac, 1736, by Benjamin Franklin. This saying isn't about God. It says we should take care of things ourselves because God isn't going to help. This is not only non-Biblical, but anti-Biblical. Leviticus 19:9-10, Matthew 25:31-46, and many other passages encourage us to help people in need rather than tell them to help themselves. This saying, however, discourages helping others, as if self-reliance can fix any problem and is our only hope. Much of the New Testament reiterates the futility in trying to live life on our own, apart from God.

Notes:

Notes:

It's also attributed to an Aesop fable in which a man with a stuck wagon prays to Hercules for help. Hercules appears and tells the man to get out and push, because "The gods help those who help themselves."

"God works in mysterious ways." Not in the Bible. It's a paraphrase of the opening line from the poem "Light Shining out of the Darkness," by William Cowper (1731-1800): "God moves in a mysterious way / His wonders to perform." The Bible does, however, repeatedly affirm that God's ways are mysterious—unknowable—to us. Ephesians 1:7-10, 3:3-5, Colossians 1:27. That's why the psalmist prays as he does in Psalm 25:4.

"Love the sinner, hate the sin." Not in the Bible. It's a paraphrase of a comment by St. Augustine in A.D. 424: "With love for mankind and hatred of sins." Also from Gandhi's 1929 autobiography: "hate the sin and not the sinner." The intent behind the saying is Biblically sound. See Romans 12:9 and Mark 12:31. This saying is a point of contention between conservative and liberal Christians. Each group seems to say the other group overemphasizes one half of the saying while underemphasizing the other half.

"Money is the root of all evil." Not in the Bible. It's a misquote of 1 Timothy 6:10, which says the "the love of money is a root of all kinds of evil" (NRSV). Big difference!

"Pride goes before a fall." Not in the Bible. It's a paraphrase of Proverbs 16:18: "Pride goes before destruction, and a haughty spirit before a fall" (NRSV).

"Spare the rod, spoil the child." Not in the Bible. This is a paraphrase of Proverbs 13:24: "Those who spare the rod hate their children, but those who love them are diligent to discipline them" (NRSV). The "rod" is the same as in Psalm 23, used to guide rather than spank. This proverb encourages teaching, guiding, and directing children, not spanking them as many take it.

"This, too, shall pass." Not in the Bible. It's possibly a paraphrase of 2 Corinthians 4:17, but just as likely a non-religious way of saying "hang in there."

Theological Underpinnings
A recent survey in the United Kingdom found rampant ignorance of the Bible in youth and children. Less than a third knew what Good Friday commemorates (although that's not necessarily in the Bible). Only one-fourth knew what Easter celebrates. Judas being Jesus' betrayer was known by 75%, but only 33% knew about that kiss. More than a third of children thought "The Tortoise and the Hare" was in the Bible. Why so much ignorance? Well, this same study revealed that 71% of parents with kids 3-16 said their children had never read, seen, or heard the Easter story. If they're not teaching their kids that story from the Bible, it's a safe bet they're not teaching them anything from the Bible.

But that's overseas. American kids are much more Bible-literate, right? Well, during Lent of 2014, a North Carolina church staged a passion play. They built and used an outdoor set of a tomb, complete with costumed Roman soldiers standing guard. According to the pastor, passers-by kept asking if they were reenacting a scene from the movie *Gladiator*.

Biblical ignorance is even a problem within the Church. We hear something that sounds old and wise, and assume it's Biblical especially if the saying reinforces what we already believe, such as "God moves in mysterious ways." Sadly, many people who claim a love for the Bible don't read it. Their exposure to scripture is limited to Sunday school and worship or quick devotionals with very little scripture. Thus, bits of folk wisdom and old sayings end up taking on Biblical authority in their lives. This puts the person in control of (presumed) scripture instead of allowing scripture—or, more precisely, the Holy Spirit working through scripture—to be their "authoritative guide for Christian living" (CP Confession of Faith 1.05).

Applying the Lesson to Your Own Life
Which guides your life and decisions more: old sayings or Holy Scripture? If you answered "scripture," are you sure your favorite, guiding passages really are from the scriptures? Which are you more likely to quote in public, scripture or an old saying?

What are some old sayings that you find timelessly true? What are some you find ridiculously outdated (not the language, but the message)? For these latter ones, were they ever true, or were they wishful thinking?

Recall a time when you realized that one of your long-held beliefs about something being in the Bible was wrong.

Notes:

Notes:

How did you respond? Did the way you approach scripture change?

Consider making a list of Bible-sounding, but not Biblical, sayings that you often hear, and then search scripture to find an actual verse that says the same thing. Next time someone uses the non-Biblical saying around you, you can respond with, "Or as the Bible says…" and see where the conversation goes.

The Lesson

Get Started (10 min.)

As soon as all students have arrived, announce that you're giving a pop quiz. Ham it up by saying the church session wants to know how well you're doing as a teacher (which, technically, should be true), or that you're thinking about starting to give grades for this class, like in school (you just thought about it, so this isn't a lie either).

Hand out pens and copies of "Is This in the Bible?" Pop Quiz, but have them keep the quiz face down.

Announce that students have 90 seconds to complete the quiz. Have students turn over their sheets, write their name on it, and begin. Every 15 seconds, call out the time remaining. When 90 seconds is up, call out "Pens down!" and collect the quizzes. Without revealing the correct answers—all the answers are "no"—grade the quizzes in front of the class and announce each student's grades. When all grades have been announced, reveal the correct answers and the fact that you've been kidding about the grades.

Ask: **Are you surprised? Which of these did you really think had to be in the Bible? Which of these did you know right away wasn't in the Bible? If these things aren't in the Bible, where do they come from?**

Explain that in this lesson the class will explore some of the things people mistakenly think are in the Bible. But first hand out the sealed envelopes with the "Is This in the Bible?" Pop Quiz copies inside. Explain that there is a copy of the quiz in each envelope and that the students are to find someone an elder, parent, grandparent, pastor, teacher —to give the quiz to in the coming week. Remind them to have a pen handy and keep the quiz sealed until someone is ready to take it. Students are to report back at the next meeting what happened.

Listen Up (20 min.)

Distribute the "That's Not In the Bible?" handouts. Work through the lists however you wish. You could go straight down the list, or pre-select which ones to discuss. You could ask students which items draw their interest, or which they're most familiar with.

Use the background information above, under "Explaining the Bible," and the discussion questions below to help you lead the discussion of each item chosen. Have a student look up and read aloud the indicated scripture, if there is one, for each item discussed.

Possible discussion questions for each item covered:

- Why do you think people think this is in the Bible, and why has it stuck?

- Have you ever heard anybody say that this is in the Bible? In real life? In a movie/TV show?

    Did you believe them? Why or why not?

- Who is most likely to believe these things are in the Bible: church-going, Bible-reading people, or people who don't read the Bible?

- What can we as a class do to teach people that this isn't from the Bible?

Notes:

Notes:

Now What? (15 min.)

Divide the class into small groups of two or three students each.

Give each group a pad of paper, a pen, and a Bible. Explain that each group is to come up with a new saying that sounds like it comes from the Bible. They can completely make up something, paraphrase a real Bible verse or Biblical concept, combine two Bible verses or concepts, or anything else they want.

The saying should be short and easy to remember. But let's avoid making any more of those Biblical-sounding sayings that actually contradict what the Bible says. These should be phrases that actually support Biblical principles.

Give about ten minutes for groups to work, and then gather the whole class back together. Have each group share its new saying.

Groups should only give explanations about their sayings if asked because the sayings should be understandable at first hearing.

Have the whole class vote on the best of these sayings, allowing some slight editing if necessary.

Lead the whole class in repeating the new saying several times, until it is memorized.

Encourage students to use this new saying as a verbal bonus question when they give the pop quiz to someone this week. Students can reveal the source of this new saying after revealing the correct answers to their test-takers.

Live It (5 min.)

Close the lesson by saying: **A lot of things people mistakenly think are in the Bible are good advice, or uplifting, or helpful in some way. That's why people think they're from the Bible. God is the source of all good things, and all good things point to God. The Bible does too. But let's always do our best to know what's really coming from the Bible and what's just coming from people.**

Resources used: archive.org, cnn.com, dictionary.com, thetimesnews.com, What the Good Book Didn't Say by J. Stephen Lang

© 2015 Discipleship Ministry Team of the Ministry Council of the Cumberland Presbyterian Church. All Rights Reserved.

Notes:

Digging Deeper:

For almost 400 years, most English-speaking Christians read and used the same version of the Bible—the King James Version. In certain circles, anyone misquoting a Bible verse or misattributing an old saying to the Bible could count on being corrected quickly. The last 50 years or so, however, has seen dozens of new translations and paraphrases. While this new scholarship is good and makes scripture available to those who struggle with outdated language, it has also caused some confusion. Now, when someone misquotes scripture or mistakenly attributes an old saying to the Bible, they are less likely to be corrected. Others who suspect a mistake may keep quiet, thinking the speaker is quoting from an unfamiliar translation. It will be interesting to see if even more non-Biblical but Bible sounding sayings emerge because of this and are passed on.

"Is This in the Bible?"
Pop Quiz

1. Adam and Eve ate an apple from the one tree God said not to eat from.
    ☐ Yes ☐ No

2. Satan and his demons live and rule in hell.
    ☐ Yes ☐ No

3. "God works in mysterious ways."
    ☐ Yes ☐ No

4. Baby Jesus was born in a stable and used a manger for a crib.
    ☐ Yes ☐ No

5. "This, too, shall pass."
    ☐ Yes ☐ No

Key
1. No
2. No
3. Yes
4. No
5. No

"THAT'S NOT IN THE BIBLE?!?"

These physical things and descriptions are NOT in the Bible
The serpent in the Garden of Eden was Satan. Genesis 3:1-15.
The forbidden fruit of Eden was an apple. Genesis 3:1-6.
Angels are pretty females, with wings and halos, playing the harp. Seraphim and cherubim do have wings, but aren't pretty. Isaiah 6, Ezekiel 10:20-22.
We each have a guardian angel. This idea might come from Matthew 18:10.
People become angels after dying. There is nothing like this anywhere in scripture.
Satan is red, with horns, carries a pitchfork, and lives in hell. See Matthew 25:41.
The Holy Grail. See Matthew 26:27. The Grail was a plot device for the story of King Arthur.

These events, or details of events are NOT in the Bible
A whale swallowed Jonah. See Jonah 1:17.
Baby Jesus born in a stable, and the innkeeper. Mangers are most often found in stables, but the Bible never mentions a stable. The innkeeper is never mentioned. Luke 2:6-12.
There were three wise men. Matthew 2:1-12.
Jesus in his underwear on the cross. He would have been naked. Matthew 26:35, Mark 16:24.
Saul/Paul falling off his horse when struck blind. No horse is mentioned. Acts 9:1-9.

These sayings are NOT in the Bible
"A fool and his money are soon parted."
Adapted from a poem by Thomas Tusser, 1557.
"Ask Jesus into your heart."
Salvation does come through Jesus, though. See John 3:16, Acts 16:31.
"Cleanliness is next to Godliness."
Adapted from ancient, non-Biblical Jewish writings and/or a John Wesley sermon.
"God helps those who help themselves."
Actually contradicts Leviticus 19:9-10, Matthew 25:31-46, and many other passages! Attributed to Benjamin Franklin (1736) and/or an ancient Aesop fable.
"God works in mysterious ways."
Paraphrase from a 1700s poem. The Bible does, however, repeatedly affirm that God's ways are mysterious (unknowable) to us. Ephesians 1:7-10, 3:3-5, Colossians 1:27. That's why the psalmist prays as he does in Psalm 25:4.
"Love the sinner, hate the sin."
Paraphrase of a comment by St. Augustine (A.D. 424) and Gandhi (1929). Agrees with Romans 12:9 and Mark 12:31, but not in the Bible as we say it today.
"Money is the root of all evil."
A misquote of 1 Timothy 6:10. Big difference!
"Pride goes before a fall."
A paraphrase of Proverbs 16:18.
"Spare the rod, spoil the child."
Paraphrase of Proverbs 13:24. Misused to condone spanking children.
"This, too, shall pass."
Possibly a paraphrase of 2 Corinthians 4:17, but just as likely a non-religious way of saying "hang in there."

Common Sayings That Come From the Bible
by Andy McClung

Scripture: Varied

Theme: Many everyday sayings have their origin in the Bible.

Resource List

- Adequate space for an active game
- Copy of "Hey, That's From the Bible" handout for each student
- Bibles, one per student

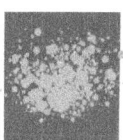

Leader Prep

- Prepare index cards as detailed below

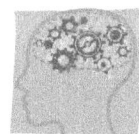

Leader Insight

Connecting to Your Students

Your students have probably been told many times to read their Bibles. They may have been told that the answers to all of life's problems are in the Bible. It's less likely, however, that they've been taught how to read the Bible. Expecting the Bible to read like a novel or FAQ list leads to frustration.

Students normally encounter the Bible in short passages in worship, Sunday school, youth group, or devotional books and then experience a much longer sermon or lesson. Students, then, experience many more words from a teacher or preacher than from scripture itself. Furthermore, the church neglects to teach that reading scripture is listening for God, while also failing to emphasize that every passage is part of some bigger work.

This lesson will not mend this deficiency in contemporary Christian education, but it will highlight some of the bite-sized sayings from the Bible that both churched and non-churched people have found helpful.

Notes:

Explaining the Topic

Presented here is the same information from the handout, but with additional notes to help you lead the discussion during the "Listen Up" portion of this lesson. This section, then, is longer than usual. Don't worry, you don't have to cover all of this information.

There are three categories of sayings (words or phrases) that this lesson covers: 1) common sayings that have their source in the Bible, but are not exact quotes, 2) common sayings that are exact (or almost exact) quotes from a particular translation of the Bible, and 3) English words and phrases that appeared in print for the very first time within an early printing of the Bible.

Common Sayings that Reference the Bible

A leopard can't change its spots—People aren't going to change. Comes from the prophet's call to change our ways, even though doing good after a life of sin is really difficult (Jeremiah 13:23).

A little bird told me—A way to say "I heard something" without revealing the source of your news. Comes from Ecclesiastes 10:20.

Armageddon—A final or epic battle, or an event so destructive it seems like the end of the world. Comes from an unknown site where the end of the world will begin with battles and all sorts of horrible things. Some translations use Har-Megiddo, which means Mountain/Hill of Megiddo. Megiddo is an ancient city where many horrible battles were fought, but it is flat land. Har-Megiddo may just mean "strong hill" and not refer to a specific place. Revelation 16:16 is the one and only mention of this word in the Bible.

Forbidden fruit—Something that's desirable, but off limits. Comes from the yummy-looking fruit on the tree in Eden, which God said not to eat. Often used to describe something bad for you (Genesis 2:16, 3:6a).

Going the extra mile—Doing more than required or expected. As a conquered nation, Jewish folks were required by Roman law to carry a Roman soldier's bag one mile whenever requested. Jesus said to carry it an additional mile as well (Matthew 5:41).

Good Samaritan—A person who helps someone in trouble with no expectation of reward. Comes from Jesus' parable of the Good Samaritan. In the parable, a Samaritan was the last person expected to provide help to a Jewish person. This factor has been subtly dropped from the common saying (Luke 10:30-35).

He/she can read the writing on the wall—Someone can tell by observation that an end is near (job, relationship, etc.). Comes from when God used a phantom hand to write on a wall to tell King Belshazzar that his reign would soon end (Daniel 5). Also, when used as "the writing is on the wall," can mean something is obvious.

Jezebel—An evil or scheming woman. Comes from Israelite queen, Jezebel, who worshiped idols and schemed to kill Israelite prophets (1 & 2 Kings). There is a website, jezebel.com, that proudly focuses on racy Hollywood news for women.

Judas—To call someone "Judas" is to say they are a betrayer. Comes from Judas Iscariot, who betrayed Jesus (Matthew 26:14-16).

Left hand doesn't know what right hand is doing—Usually used negatively today to mean uncoordinated actions within the same organization, especially when those actions impede each other. The term can also be used to imply underhanded deeds done in secret. It was originally positive, as Paul encouraged anonymity in generosity and good deeds (Matthew 6:3).

Talent—Originally a sum of money, but now an ability or skill. Definition change occurred in 1300s because so many preachers used Matthew 25:14-30 to make a point about using God-given skills/abilities in a way that pleases God. Tearing your hair out—To agonize over something. Comes from Ezra 9:3.

United we stand, divided we fall—self-explanatory. When Jesus was accused of being from Satan, he said "No city or house divided against itself will stand," meaning that if he was from Satan he wouldn't be working against Satan (Matthew 12:25).

You don't know the half of it—A way to say there's a lot more to be known. Used by Queen of Sheba to Solomon. 1 Kings 10:6-7.

Notes:

Notes:

Common Sayings That Are (Almost) Exact Quotes from the Bible

Nothing but skin and bones—underfed, really skinny (Job 19:19-20).

Give to Caesar what is Caesar's—multiple meanings, but mainly means give what is rightfully due. When said by Jesus, it was followed with, "and to God what is God's," to emphasize that eternal things are more important than temporal things (Matthew 22:21).

The powers that be—those who are in charge (Romans 13:1). A man after [my] own heart—someone who thinks like me and desires the same things I do (1 Samuel 13:14).

Apple of my eye—special, particularly beloved. Deuteronomy 32:10, Psalm 17:8, Zechariah 2:8.

At their wit's end—at the limit of their mental resources, don't know what to do next (Psalm 107:27).

Blind leading the blind—Someone who doesn't know what they're doing telling others what to do (Matthew 15:14, Luke 6:39).

Drop in the bucket—an insignificant or inconsequential amount to what is needed, or a comparison to say something is so small as to not even register (Isaiah 40:15).

An eye for an eye—revenge, repaying an injury with an equal injury. Exodus 21:24, Leviticus 24:20, Deuteronomy 19:21. Originally meant to instill fair punishment for crimes, however, it became a rule used for revenge. Notice, however, that in Matthew 5:38-39, Jesus reveals a better way to act when harmed.

How the mighty have fallen—used to note someone's loss of power or prestige, usually due to some moral failure (1 Samuel 2:19-27).

Labor of love—work done for interest in the work rather than for payment (1 Thessalonians 1:3).

Letter of the law—the impersonal, literal interpretation of law, usually used in contrast to spirit, intent, of the law. Paul used it to condemn the Pharisaical interpretation of God's law (2 Corinthians 3:6).

Pride goes before a fall—stuck up folks end up being humbled (Proverbs 16:19).

Present in spirit—used with "but not in body." A way to say you're thinking about someone when not with them physically (Colossians 2:5).

Rise and shine—wake up, get out of bed. Originally: let God's glory shine through you (Isaiah 60:1).

Salt of the earth—used in reference to a person(s) to say they're good folks (honest, hard-working, dependable, etc.) Used by Jesus to say how important we are (Matthew 5:13).

Scapegoat—someone to place the blame on. Originally, an actual goat (Azazel) upon which the sins of an entire village were ceremonially placed before it was sent to its death outside of the encampment (Leviticus 16:9-10).

Stranger in a strange land—someone really out of place, far out of their comfort zone. Originally referred to Moses (Exodus 2: 22).

Sweat of your brow—hard work (Genesis 3:19).

Twinkling of an eye—really quickly (1 Corinthians 15:52).

English Words/Phrases Whose First In-print Appearance was in the Bible

Included here are just a few words, chosen for their potential interest to youth, which entered the English language because someone used them in early English versions of the Bible. Other words may have appeared in partial translations earlier, but these first appeared in print in complete translations.

Inclusion here does not mean these words were invented for use in an English Bible. Most were adapted from Latin, some from Greek or Hebrew. It makes sense that some English words first appeared in print in a Bible, because the Bible was one of the earliest books to be printed in English, and certainly the most printed. For each entry, the date and version of the Bible it first appeared in are given, as well as the passage in which it appeared.

These may not be as ripe for discussion as the other phrases in this lesson, but do at least draw your students' attention to them.

Notes:

Notes:

Adoption. Romans 8:23. 1382, Wycliffe.

Appetite, when used to express desire for something other than food. Ezekiel 21:16. 1382, Wycliffe.

Bald head. 2 Kings 2:23. 1535, Coverdale.

Beautiful. Matthew 23:27. 1525, Tyndale.

Blab, meaning to talk a lot about nothing. Proverbs 15:2. 1535, Coverdale.

Crime. Acts 23:29. 1382, 1382, Wycliffe.

Doubtful. Ezekiel 12:24. 1388, Wycliffe (revised).

Female. Genesis 1:27. 1382, Wycliffe.

Horror. Deuteronomy 32:10. 1382, Wycliffe.

Infidel. 2 Corinthians 6:15. 1525, Tyndale.

Liberty. 2 Corinthians 3:17. 1382, Wycliffe.

Mystery, meaning something known only through divine revelation. Romans 16:25. 1382, Wycliffe.

Mystery, meaning something unknown and to be figured out. Daniel 2:27. 1382, Wycliffe.

Network. Exodus 27:4. 1560, Geneva Bible.

Puberty. Malachi 2:14. 1382, Wycliffe.

Sex, meaning gender. Genesis 6:19. 1382, Wycliffe.

Wrinkle. Ephesians 5:27. 1420, Wycliffe (revised).

Theological Underpinnings
It shocks some long-time Christians to learn that the Bible wasn't first written in English. Hopefully, though, your students already know better. (They will if you've used the Faith Out Loud Lesson "How'd We Get the Bible, Anyway?" from Volume 1, Quarter 1.)

Even the word "Bible" isn't an original English word. It comes from the Greek word for book. Thus, we could call any book a "bible." That's why the covers and title pages of many Bibles say "Holy Bible," which means "holy book." In English, we also distinguish the Holy Bible by capitalizing the word "bible," with or without including the word "holy."

When you look at the big picture, English and scripture came together only recently. Copies of scripture in Hebrew were in use about 1,000 B.C. By 500 B.C. the Torah (Genesis-Deuteronomy) had been translated into Aramaic.

The Old Testament was translated into Greek about 250 B.C. The New Testament, in Greek, became official about A.D. 350. In A.D. 405 the whole Bible was translated into Latin. It wasn't for another 977 years that the whole Bible was translated into English. This was done by John Wycliffe and his followers.

The Holy Bible is indeed our "authoritative guide for Christian living" as our Confession of Faith says (1.05). English speakers should never forget, however that we were invited to participate in Bible reading long after many others, and even then, not by our merit, but only by God's grace.

Applying the Lesson to Your Own Life
Without reading further, can you name some common sayings with Biblical origins? How many of these do people of your generation use regularly? How many of these do/did people of your parents' and grandparents' generations use regularly?

When you read the Bible, do you read entire chapters or books in one sitting, or just a few verses? Why? In worship, do you prefer the preacher or liturgist to read short passages or long passages of scripture? Why?

How might you respond if someone said the Bible isn't relevant to real life?

As you prepare to lead this lesson, take note of any common sayings that you didn't know had Biblical origins. Be sure to share these with your students, and others, later on.

Notes:

Notes:

The Lesson

Get Started (10 min.)

If your classroom is too small for all students to be on their feet and moving around, consider moving this part, or the whole lesson, outdoors or to another room.

Well before class, prepare several pairs of index cards by writing the first part of a common saying on one card and the remainder of the saying on the other card (see below). To make this exercise easier, add ellipses (...) after the first part of the saying and before the remainder of the saying. To make this exercise harder, leave these off and don't use ending punctuation on the second card of each pair.

Sayings for index cards:
Forbidden ... fruit
How the mighty ... have fallen
The blind leading ... the blind.
Give to Caesar ... what is Caesar's
Nothing but skin ... and bones
Apple of ... my eye
Scape ... goat
At my wit's ... end
A leopard can't ... change its spots
A drop ... in a bucket
An eye ... for an eye
Signs of... the times
The truth shall ... make you free
United we stand ... divided we fall
The twinkling ... of an eye
A man after ... my own heart
Rise and ... shine
Stranger in ... a strange land
Absent in body ... but present in spirit
You don't know ... the half of it

Option #1 (For a class with more than 8 students, or to make the exercise take less time):

As a subtle hint, you could use several different colors of ink to make the cards, and ensure that both parts of each saying are written in the same color. If you do this, don't point it out unless someone is really stumped.

It's better to have too many cards than not enough, so make plenty. Keep the pairs together in case you need to discard some after you know how many students will be playing. If you have an odd number of students, you'll need to play the game as well.

After all students have arrived, make sure you have the appropriate number of card pairs, and then thoroughly shuffle the cards.

Explain the game: **Well-known sayings are written on these cards, half on one card and half on another. Your job is to take a card and find the person whose card completes the saying on yours. When you've found him or her, stand still side-by-side and hold up your cards.**

Distribute the cards, one per student. You can distribute them by handing each student a card, having each student pick an unseen card, or tossing the whole stack into the air and having students grab for them.

When time is up or when all card pairs have been matched, have students read aloud the complete)sayings on their cards.

Then ask: **What do all these saying have in common?** (They all come from the Bible.)

Transition into the rest of the lesson by saying: **Whether or not the people using them know it, a lot of the familiar "old sayings" we use come from the Bible.**

Notes:

Notes:

Option #2 (For a class with 8 or fewer students, or to make the exercise take more time):

Use a lot of cards, far more than one per student. Shuffle the cards thoroughly. Divide students into two teams. (Everybody who's had pizza in the last two days vs. those who haven't, those with birthday dates 1-15 vs. those with birthday dates 16-31, or some other arbitrary grouping. Teams do not have to have an equal number of students.) Assign each team a home base in opposite corners of the room.

Explain the game: **Well-known sayings are written on these cards, half on one card and half on another. Your job is to match up the two cards that complete each saying and place them side by side in your home base. You may only take matched pairs to your home base, not single cards.**

Toss the cards into the air, and let them fall to the floor. Then say: Go!

When time is up or when all card pairs have been matched, have students read aloud the complete sayings on their cards.

Then ask: **What do all these saying have in common?** (They all come from the Bible.)

Transition into the rest of the lesson by saying: **Whether or not the people using them know it, a lot of the familiar "old sayings" we use come from the Bible.**

Listen Up (20 min.)

Distribute the "Hey, That's From the Bible" handouts. Work through the sayings however you wish. You could go straight down the list, or pre-select which ones to discuss. You could ask students which sayings draw their interest, or which they've heard and which they haven't.

Use the background information above, under "Explaining the Bible," and the discussion questions below to help you lead the discussion of each saying chosen. For each saying discussed, have a student look up and read aloud the indicated scripture.

Possible discussion questions for each saying covered:

- Why do you think this saying caught on and stuck, when thousands of others didn't?
- Have you ever heard anybody say this? In real life? In a movie/TV show? Did you understand what they meant, or did you have to ask?
- What age person is most likely to use this saying?
- Who is most likely to use this saying: a church-going, Bible-reading person, or someone who just knows it from culture?
- Does this saying still mean the same thing it meant in the Bible? If not, why do you think it changed?

Now What? (15 min.)

Detailed below are two options to use with this part of the lesson. As time permits, and according to your students' anticipated degree of participation, you could use one or both of them.

Improv Theatre

Choose two students, and have them stand in front of the class. Explain that you are going to give them a setting/situation, and they are to carry on a conversation as if in that setting/situation. Their goal is to make the conversation believable, but also to bring in one of the sayings that has been mentioned in class. Whichever student is the first to work in one of these sayings appropriately gets to pick another student to take his/her place, dictate the next setting/situation, and then sit down. Keep playing until time runs out, everyone has had a turn, or it's no longer fun. Encourage students to pick others who haven't had a turn.

Notes:

Notes:

Possible settings/situations, in case a student can't think of one:

- he's asking her out on a date but she doesn't want to go
- a parent trying to get a teen to clean up his/her room
- a customer trying to buy something from a clerk, but customer can't remember the name of the product
- two students gossiping about why another student was called to the principal's office
- in the locker room, after the game
- talking about the latest best seller/blockbuster/chart topper
- wondering what's going on behind a closed door
- a driving test

Create a Saying

Have students gather in groups of two or three. Give each group a Bible.

Tell them to think of some Bible story or passage of scripture and come up with a new saying from that story or passage. It does not have to be a direct quote, but should somehow relate back to the story or passage.

(Example: A new saying for when someone does something seemingly impossible or extremely difficult could be, "That's some water to wine, right there!" from John 2:1-11.)

Bring all groups back together to share their new sayings. Have students vote on one to try to make viral or catch on. Each student will use this saying several times and in different settings during the week, in person, on the phone, texting, and on social media.

It will be interesting to listen/watch and find out if the saying has caught on.

Live It (5 min.)

Say: **Lots of people say the Bible doesn't make sense, or it's just not relevant to real life. Well, all these sayings have been around so long because people have found them to be very relevant and very helpful. And they all come from the Bible so, that shows us the Bible does make sense and is relevant.**

Encourage students to listen for anyone using one of these sayings in the coming weeks. When they hear someone using one, challenge them to say, "Did you know that comes from the Bible?" and see where the Holy Spirit leads the conversation from there.

Resources used: bartleby.com, Coined by God by Stanley Malless and Jeffrey McQuain, entymonline.com, dictionary.com, the freedictionary.com, The New Bible Dictionary

© 2015 Discipleship Ministry Team of the Ministry Council of the Cumberland Presbyterian Church. All Rights Reserved.

Notes:

About the contributors...

Rev. Melissa R. Goodloe earned her M.Div (2005) at Memphis Theological Seminary. Melissa is the pastor of the Shiloh Cumberland Presbyterian Church near McKenzie, Tennessee. She and her husband Tim reside in the Macedonia community with their two dogs, two cats, and a school of fish.

Rev. Dr. Andy McClung has been teaching Cumberland Presbyterian youth and adults since 1988, both in person and through his writing. A double graduate of Memphis Theological Seminary (M.Div., 1994 and D.Min., 2002), Andy has served congregations in Alabama, Arkansas, Mississippi, and Tennessee. Cursed with a dry sense of humor and blessed with a love for the Cumberland Presbyterian Church, he lives in Memphis and continues to teach, preach, write, and serve the church at the presbyterial, synodic, and denominational levels.

Rev. T.J. Malinoski is in charge of Evangelism and New Church Development at the denominational level of the Cumberland Presbyterian Church. He is a graduate of Bethel College and Memphis Theological Seminary and has served congregations in Alabama and Tennessee. His sermons and writings have been featured in the *Cumberland Presbyterian*, *Missionary Messenger*, and *Alabama Living* magazines.

Series editor for **Faith Out Loud** is Nathan Wheeler. Line editor is Mark A. Taylor. Electronic processing and incidental layout by Matthew H. Gore. **Faith Out Loud** logo and cover design are by Joanna Wilkinson. Produced for the Discipleship Ministry Team of the Ministry Council of the Cumberland Presbyterian Church.